CHAUCER

Peter Ackroyd is the biographer of T.S. Eliot, Dickens, Blake and Thomas More, and the author of *London: The Biography* and *Albion: The Origins of the English Imagination*. His recent novel, *The Clerkenwell Tales*, is set in medieval London at the time of Chaucer. Peter Ackroyd lives in London, and in 2003 was awarded a CBE for his services to literature.

ALSO BY PETER ACKROYD

Fiction

The Great Fire of London
The Last Testament of Oscar Wilde
Hawksmoor
Chatterton
First Light
English Music
The House of Doctor Dee
Dan Leno and the Limehouse Golem
Milton in America
The Plato Papers
The Clerkenwell Tales
The Lambs of London

Non-Fiction

*Dressing Up: Transvestism and Drag:
The History of an Obsession*
London: The Biography
Albion: The Origins of the English Imagination
Illustrated London

Biography

Ezra Pound and his World
T.S. Eliot
Dickens
Blake
The Life of Thomas More

Poetry

Ouch!
The Diversions of Purley and other Poems

Criticism

Notes for a New Culture
*The Collection: Journalism, Reviews, Essays, Short Stories,
Lectures* edited by Thomas Wright

Peter Ackroyd

CHAUCER

Brief Lives

V

VINTAGE

Published by Vintage 2005

2 4 6 8 10 9 7 5 3 1

Copyright © Peter Ackroyd 2004

Peter Ackroyd has asserted his right under the Copyright, Designs and Patents Act, 1988 to be identified as the author of this work

First published in Great Britain in 2004 by
Chatto & Windus

Vintage
Random House, 20 Vauxhall Bridge Road,
London SW1V 2SA

Random House Australia (Pty) Limited
20 Alfred Street, Milsons Point, Sydney
New South Wales 2061, Australia

Random House New Zealand Limited
18 Poland Road, Glenfield,
Auckland 10, New Zealand

Random House (Pty) Limited
Endulini, 5A Jubilee Road, Parktown 2193,
South Africa

The Random House Group Limited Reg. No. 954009
www.randomhouse.co.uk/vintage

A CIP catalogue record for this book
is available from the British Library

ISBN 0 099 28748 X

Papers used by Random House are natural, recyclable products made from wood grown in sustainable forests. The manufacturing processes conform to the environmental regulations of the country of origin

Printed and bound in Great Britain by
Cox & Wyman Limited, Reading, Berkshire

Contents

List of Illustrations

21   Chaucer's tomb in Poets' Corner, Westminster Abbey. From a nineteenth-century aquatint. The Stapleton Collection/BAL

Colour Section

Edward III and his son Edward Prince of Wales ('The Black Prince'). British Library/AKG

John of Gaunt dining with the King of Portugal. Fifteenth-century artist of the English school. British Library/BAL

'The Garden of Love.' European, fifteenth century. Giraudon/BAL

John of Gaunt. BAL

The boy king Richard II holding court after his coronation. By Jan de Batard Wavrin. 1387. BAL

William Blake's engraving of Chaucer and the Canterbury pilgrims, 1810. BAL

Boccaccio. Detail from 'The Duke of Berry receiving a manuscript from Boccaccio'. French school, fifteenth century. Bibliotheque Nationale/BAL

Petrarch. From the frescoes of famous men and women at the Villa Carducci, *c.*1450. Giraudon/BAL

Dante by Sandro Botticelli (1444/5–1510). BAL

The weighing of wool. Fifteenth-century manuscript. Venice, Museo Civico Correr/AKG

Anne of Bohemia, queen of Richard II, dying of plague. British Library/BAL

Portrait of Chaucer, from the poem 'Regement of the Princes' by Thomas Hoccleve (*c.*1368–1426). British Library/BAL

Portrait of Chaucer from the frontispiece to *Troilus and Criseyde*. It shows him reading or reciting to the court of

Richard II. Corpus Christi College, Cambridge/BAL (also reproduced in black and white opposite the Prologue)
Portrait of Chaucer from the Ellesmere manuscript of *The Canterbury Tales*. Huntington Library and Art Gallery/BAL
Details from *The Canterbury Tales*: the Monk and his greyhounds, the Cook, the Squire and the Friar. Huntington Library and Art Gallery/BAL

The author and the publishers are grateful to the Bridgeman Art Library (BAL) and akg-images (AKG) for assistance with picture research.

Family tree showing the three English kings (Edward III, Richard II and Henry IV) and the two English princes (Lionel, Duke of Clarence, and John of Gaunt) for whom Chaucer worked

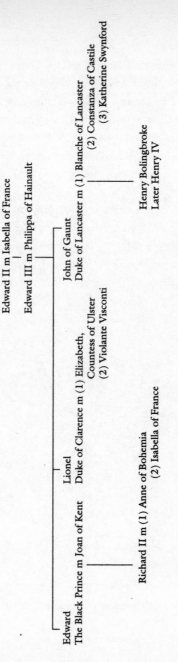

Chaucer addressing the court of Richard II. See also colour section

Prologue

There is an image of Geoffrey Chaucer, in early middle age, addressing a small audience of courtiers; he is standing on an enclosed platform (see opposite) with a richly embroidered tapestry draped across its rails. It is not a pulpit but Chaucer has raised his right hand in preacherly attitude; it is commonly assumed that he is reciting from his poetry, but no book is clearly visible. This picture forms the painted frontispiece for one manuscript copy of *Troilus and Criseyde*; it was executed in the early fifteenth century, but the portrait of Chaucer himself appears to have been copied from earlier originals. He has a forked beard, a moustache, and copious brown hair.

It may also be noticed here that his height is commonly estimated to have been five feet and six inches, average for the period, and that by his own testimony he was portly to the point of being plump. He is not depicted in the clerkly robe of the learned poet but, rather, in the fashionable dress of a courtier. This should be emphasised as one of the most significant aspects of Chaucer's art. From the age of fourteen until the very end of his life, he remained in royal service. He was a familiar and indispensable part of the court, and acted as a royal servant for three kings and two princes. That is why the border of this frontispiece is composed of entwined leaves and flowers, in recognition of the playful distinction at the court between the followers of the leaf, the practitioners of chaste '*fine amour*', and the followers of the flower who engage in the worldly pursuit of '*plaisaunce*'. Chaucer's early verse was part of these love games.

The audience in the picture also repays examination. The figure of Richard II can be clearly seen, in golden robes, and it is significant that Chaucer should be so notably associated with him. Richard, who reigned from 1377 to 1399, was perhaps the most interesting and mysterious of English sovereigns. He was a king devoted to majesty and magnificence, in an age when feudal authority was in retreat. The very circumstances of the portrait, for example, emphasise the theatricality of poetic exposition in a culture possessed by an essentially dramatic vision. The vivid colour of the frontispiece (see colour plates) is also an aspect of its drama, since colour was seen in highly allegorical terms: yellow was the colour of jealousy, blue of fidelity, while green was a token of disloyalty. The fourteenth century has been dubbed 'an age in transition', but all ages are in transition. The difference is that Chaucer came to maturity in a period when the evidence of change was all around him. His own fragmented and discontinuous work, *The Canterbury Tales,* is itself one indication.

Other figures, within this royal court gathered in a private park, have also been identified with varying degrees of certainty. Richard's consort, Queen Anne, has been glimpsed; Chaucer's first and most enduring patron, John of Gaunt, has also been seen among the press of courtiers. It has largely gone unremarked, however, that the audience is composed primarily of women. They were seen to be the natural audience for tales and romances of every kind. In succeeding centuries, in fact, the audience for the novel was deemed to be principally female. This may also provide a clue to the tone of Chaucer's early and most courtly poetry.

Yet some of the women here do not seem to be listening to Chaucer; the apparently rapt attention of others could also be interpreted as boredom or bewilderment. By indirection this touches upon the nature of artistic invention in the period; it was attentive to the minute and individual details of depicted life. The portrait, like the art of Chaucer himself, is able to provide the illusion of a group in volumetric space together with the delicate rendition of such detail. Yet this passion for realism, if the anachronism may be permitted, is accompanied by the mystery of the overall form. The portrait of Chaucer addressing his audience is surmounted by the image of a procession beside the walls of a medieval castle, yet the meaning of this scene is unclear. Some believe that it illustrates a passage from *Troilus and Criseyde* itself; others suppose that it depicts a group of courtiers arriving at Chaucer's recital, with the poet himself prominent among them.

Geoffrey Chaucer was a poet, but he was also a diplomat and an official who at various times supervised the building works of the king and the custom tariffs at the Port of London. He was appointed as a judge and as a Member of Parliament. He was a Londoner who found a natural audience among rich and influential London merchants, but he was also an enthusiast for French and Italian poetry. He excelled in translation. He is best known for *The Canterbury Tales*, but that work was composed towards the end of his poetic career. He had previously written dream visions, animal fables, moral legends and a long poem, *Troilus and Criseyde*, which has been described somewhat loosely as the first modern novel. He was prolific and various, accomplished and ingenious. He has been described as 'the father of English poetry', but he is a most perplexing parent. He professed himself to be bookish, but he was committed to an active and successful life in the world. He presented himself as reserved and quiet, but he was sued for debt and accused of rape. He is best known as the secular writer of parodies and sexual farces, but he was also possessed by a profound religious vision. Out of these contrasts, perhaps, a coherent picture may eventually emerge.

Chapter One
The Londoner

Chaucer grew up, and found his true place, in what he called 'our citee'. He was born, in the phrase of Oscar Wilde, into the purple of London commerce. He did not need to rise through his own individual effort because his position in urban society was comfortable and assured.

His paternal grandparents had come from Ipswich to London, part of that steady influx into the city from the Midlands and East Anglia; London had become the vortex for mercantile activity. His grandfather, Robert le Chaucer, was a mercer who like his grandson eventually entered the king's service; there was a strong affinity between trade and the court. He was also known as Robert Malyn, the surname meaning 'astute'. That was another characteristic he bequeathed to his famous scion. The derivation of 'Chaucer' is more uncertain. It may come from chauffecire, to seal with hot wax in the manner of a clerk, but it is more likely to derive from chaussier or shoemaker and hosier. But this in itself has little to do with Chaucer's family – Robert le Chaucer acquired his name from his quondam master, a mercer named John le Chaucer who was killed in the course of a brawl.

The poet's father, John Chaucer, was a successful and influential vintner, or wine merchant, who also entered royal service; he was part of Edward III's abortive expedition against Scotland in 1327, and eventually became deputy butler to the king's household. In his early youth he was kidnapped by some agents for his aunt and forcibly removed to Ipswich, to take part in a marriage advantageous to that lady, but the aunt was sued and despatched to the Marshalsea prison. It is a bizarre episode but serves only to confirm the sporadic lawlessness and violence of fourteenth-century life. Chaucer's maternal grandfather, John de Copton, was murdered in 1313 close to his house in Aldgate. The city records reveal that murder, abduction and rape were commonplace; at a later date, as we shall see, Chaucer himself was accused of rape. Agnes de Copton, Chaucer's mother, was a notable addition to the Chaucer family; she was an heiress, owner of many tenements and of acres in Stepney; in addition she was niece and ward of the Keeper of the Royal Mint.

Geoffrey Chaucer first saw the light, therefore, in a wealthy and influential household. The date of his birth is not certainly known but all the available evidence suggests some time between 1341 and 1343. There is some evidence of a sister, named Katherine, but no contemporaneous record of siblings has been found. He was born in an upper chamber of the family house in Thames Street, which ran parallel to the river in the ward of Vintry, which of course was the district of the wine merchants. The house itself was commodious and well proportioned; in the records it is described as stretching from the river in the south to the stream called the Walbrook in the north, into which all the household refuse was dumped. Anyone who understands the topography of London will realise that this was indeed a large house, which must have possessed a sizeable garden stretching down to the Walbrook at the back. It contained cellars in which the barrels of wine were stored after being unloaded from the wharves a few yards away. On the ground floor, above the cellars and looking out upon the street, was a chamber which acted as his father's business premises; behind it there would have been a hall, in which the more formal aspects of familial life were conducted. There would have been upper chambers, a kitchen and larder, a privy and perhaps garret rooms.

The neighbourhood itself reflected the solidity and prosperity of the house. It encompassed the dwellings of other rich vintners, some of them with their own courtyards, but it was not necessarily a fashionable area. It was a place of work and commerce. There were several lanes and alleys leading down from Thames Street to the riverside and, in particular, to Three Cranes Wharf where the wines of Gascony were unloaded. A little to the west was Queenhithe to which fish and salt, fuel and corn, were brought in a variety of ships. Chaucer would have known intimately these clamorous thoroughfares – Simpson's Lane, Spittle Lane, Brikels Lane, Brode Lane most suitable for the passage of the carts, and Three Cranes Lane known in his childhood as Painted Tavern Lane. A few hundred yards away stood the Steelyard, the defended quarters where the German merchants lived and worked; a colony of Genoese merchants was also situated by the riverside, and it has been suggested that Chaucer's knowledge of Italian sprang from such early contacts. Certainly he came to maturity in a cosmopolitan city.

So we can imagine him standing in one of the principal

thoroughfares of London, Cheapside, which he knew all of his life. He was the poet of sunrise rather than of sunset, which is as much to say that he was medieval rather than modern, and at dawn in Cheapside the whole city would awake around him. The bell rang at the church of St Thomas of Acon, at the corner of Ironmonger Lane, on the hour before sunrise; then the wickets beside the great gates of the city were opened, and through the darkness trailed in the petty traders, the chapmen, the hucksters with baskets of gooseberries or apples, the journeymen, the labourers and the servants who lived outside the walls in the crowded and malodorous suburbs which were the city's shadow. At dawn the bells in the churches rang to proclaim the ending of the curfew, but already the majority of working citizens were awake and washed. There was a proverbial refrain:

> Rise at five, dine at nine,
> Sup at five, and bed at nine,
> Will make a man live to ninety and nine.

Cheapside was a wide thoroughfare, but also a crowded and noisy one. There were terraces of tall timber houses, rising three storeys, with their gables turned to the street; they projected over the road, and were painted in vivid colours with their framework outlined in intricate patterning. They were built upon stone foundations but were completed with timber framing as well as wattle-and-daub. There may also have been smaller dwellings, of two storeys, and perhaps even a tenement made up of single rooms further divided by partitions for poor families. Certainly these 'decaying' houses, as they were known, would have been visible along the lanes and alleys which ran off the main street. Yet Cheapside was known for its shops and its stalls of merchandise. At one end, a few yards past Old Jewry and by St Mary Woolchurch, stood the Stocks market with its fish and flesh; sited a few yards apart from it were the quarters of the poulterers. At the other end of Cheapside, close to Paternoster Row and the cathedral church of St Paul, was a large covered market in which tradesmen would sell their wares out of boxes or chests.

But the street was largely comprised of individual shops and sheds packed closely together, one for every ten feet (three metres) of road-space. Each trade had its own area so that, for example, the goldsmiths were situated between Friday Street and Bread Street; within the dim interiors Chaucer would have seen on display the spoons and phials, the rings and necklaces, the crucifixes of silver gilt and paternosters of amber or coral. Friday Street itself was named after the fish market which assembled there on that day, while Bread Street was known for its bakers and its cook-shops where ten eggs or a roast lark could be purchased for a penny and a hen baked in a pasty bought for fivepence. Just past the goldsmiths, between Friday Street and Bow Church, stood the shops of the mercers with their silks and fabrics, while opposite haberdashers sold hats and laces, boots and pen-cases. Other shops sold toys and drugs, spices and small-ware. In Paternoster Row, leading off Cheapside, were the stationers and booksellers with their psalters and calendars, doctrinals and books of physic. The signs of the different trades were suspended on poles, and there were drawings on the wooden walls of the shops as a symbol of what lay within. Most of these ground-floor shops were protected by an overhanging storey, or penthouse, where the shopkeeper and his family would live in one or two rooms. If a house boasted a small cellar or undercroft it would be utilised for storage or for trade, with ale one of the most easily available commodities.

Among the one-storey sheds and the two-storey dwellings, with whitewashed walls and thatched roofs, would be vacant plots and gardens. Down the smaller streets were shops and cottages, fences and barrels, with chickens and ducks, goats and pigs, roaming among them. Most of the pavements would have needed repair, and there were piles of refuse or manure on the streets waiting for the 'raker' or 'fermour' to remove them. The air was filled with the smell of burning wood and of sea-coal, of cess pits and butchers' waste.

At sunrise the great gates of the city were opened, and the long bakers' wagons from Mile End would bear their

Feeding the chickens, *c.* 1340

precious burden into the streets of the city; simnel bread was best, and cocket the worst. Horses and carts of every description would also begin their journey through the narrow streets among the porters and water-carriers and merchants. In a city continually expanding, there was building work everywhere. In the latter half of the fourteenth century the population of London has been variously estimated between forty thousand and fifty thousand but, whatever the density, the square mile within the walls was sufficiently noisy and active. The population of London was characteristically compared to a swarm of bees, busily engaged but when threatened dangerous and deadly. Yet the greetings upon the street, at any dawn, would have seemed beneficent enough. 'God save you . . . God give you grace . . . God's speed . . . Good day, a clear day.' Mixed with these greetings the cries of the street-sellers would already be added to the clamour and shouting which accompanied the start of each day. 'Twelve herrings for a penny! Hot pies! Good pigs and geese! Ribs of beef and many a pie!' The blind would stand on street corners with their white willow wands and sing such popular songs as 'Jay tout perdu mon temps et mon labour', which Chaucer mentions, and 'My love has fared inland'. Chaucer would have thoroughly absorbed the language of the streets, that rich polyglot mixture of Latin patois, Anglo-Norman phraseology and English demotic; it emerges in Chaucer's consistent hyperbole, so much a feature of London speech, but also in the stray phrases which are embedded in his aureate verse – 'Come of, man . . . lat se now . . . namoore of this . . . what sey ye . . . take hede now . . . Jakke fool!' At night, and in moments of relative quiet, the sound of the river would clearly be heard.

An apt symbol for the Catholic culture of fourteenth-century London might be found in the fact that there were ninety-nine churches, and ninety-five inns, within the walls. (The hermitages and oratories have not been included, but neither have the ubiquitous ale-cellars.) In future generations the piety of Londoners was recognised all over Europe, and there is no reason to suppose that the faith of the fourteenth century was any less intense. The celebration of the Mass was at the centre of London worship; the bells pealed out at that blessed moment when the bread is turned into the body of Christ and becomes the eucharist; at that moment, divine life entered and renewed urban time. It was a culture of ceremony and ritual, of hierarchy and display, modelled upon sacred typology and the liturgical year. It is not surprising, therefore, that the poetry of Chaucer is suffused with religious practice and religious personages. *The Canterbury Tales* is of course itself set within the context of a pilgrimage, and hardly one of those tales is not concerned directly or indirectly with 'hooly chirches good'. In that compendium of late medieval narratives there are saints' tales and pietistic texts. The urban parades and religious processions upon London's streets, as well as the stridently colourful dress of the citizens, also testify to a culture of spectacle and display. It is a culture in which the ideal and the real interpenetrate one another, so that the most vivid or naturalistic detail within Chaucer's poetry can be suffused with a sense of the sacred. In the mystery plays, which Chaucer would have witnessed, the events of biblical history are interrupted by farce and obscenity; in 'The Miller's Tale' of *The Canterbury Tales*, a domestic version of Noah and his ark becomes the occasion for 'fart', 'piss' and a 'naked ers'. In a civilisation where death and disease were so pressing, and so close to hand, why should there be any conception of 'good taste'?

There is a description of London in the twelfth century, written by William Fitzstephen, which furnishes the context for the development of the city in Chaucer's lifetime. He describes the meadows and springs which lay just beyond the city's bounds; even in the fourteenth century the sentinels of the city walls and gates looked out over fields, and bells were rung to call in agricultural labourers at curfew time. He mentions the 'smooth field', where horses were raced and purchased, which by Chaucer's time was known as Smythfelde; it had become the site of a market and a fair, as well as the spot where malefactors were hanged by a clump of elm-trees. It was already a city of violent contrasts. Fitzstephen describes the ancient governance of London with its wards, and sheriffs, and courts. Chaucer himself would have grown up within the network of these obligations which stretched back, in the medieval phrase, 'beyond the memory of man'.

His poetry is often conceived to be of springtime rather than of autumn, as if he believed himself to come from a freshly minted civilisation; yet London was deemed to be more ancient than Rome. Fitzstephen's account concludes with a description of the sports and games of the city. He mentions the dramatised versions of saints' legends, played out upon the streets, in the same paragraph as he alludes to the cock-fights organised by schoolboys at Shrovetide. He describes football and horse-racing, ice-skating and archery,

as well as bull-baiting and boar-baiting by savage dogs. In
the context of these violent delights, he might have
mentioned the sporadic but intense violence of Londoners
themselves; the city records are filled with reports of riots
and murderous affrays, with which Chaucer himself became
all too familiar. Fitzstephen adds that the 'only incon-
veniencies of London are, the immoderate drinking of
foolish persons, and the frequency of fires'. Since this is a
complaint repeated down the centuries, even perhaps into
our own time, then we may safely conclude that the city
itself has certain unchanging characteristics. When we read
Chaucer's poetry, then, it may speak to us directly.

From the circumstances of the fourteenth century an
eternal London vision can emerge. Chaucer is intrigued by
crowds and processions; the Canterbury pilgrims themselves
form a parade, and the figure of the 'verray, parfit gentil
knyght' might be that of St George upon one of the pageant
wagons which trundled down Cornhill and Cheapside.
Chaucer is preoccupied, also, with variety and contrast in a
world where 'high' and 'low' mingle. His poems are filled
with many competing voices, as if he were repeating the
accents of the London crowd, and his work is suffused with
a theatricality and vivacity that might derive from the
contemplation of the endlessly changing urban world.
Chaucer is in love with spectacle of every description, and
with the external life of humankind. He is a London artist.

As a child he lived beside the church of St Martin in the
Vintry, where no doubt he was baptised on the day after his
birth; beside that was a large house of stone and timber
known simply as the Vintry. Here dwelled at various times
John Gisers and Henry Picard, both vintners and both lord

mayors of London. But there were also cook-shops and taverns in the immediate vicinity, for the merchants as well as for those who worked on the wharves; the labour was most intensive between the months of April and June, when 'the wines of rack' arrived, and in November for 'the wine of vintage'. One stretch of Thames Street was known as 'cooks' row' so that, according to the sixteenth-century London antiquary John Stow, 'in those days (and till of late time) every man lived by his professed trade, not any one interrupting another: the cooks dressed meat and sold no wine, and the taverner sold wine, but dressed no meat for sale'.

The infant Chaucer was brought up in a richly furnished household. The general reports of merchants' houses suggest a fair degree of comfort; deep feather-beds, cushions, tapestries and embroidered hangings are characteristically included in any inventory of domestic effects. The modern notion of the medieval house seems to consist of cold stone,

Butchering and cooking meat, and carrying it to the table, *c.*1340

bare walls and malodorous corners, but in fact the more prosperous households would have been comfortable, colourful and clean. The wooden sideboards would be filled with silverware, an obvious token of wealth, and the walls would be decorated with tapestries or murals. The clothes of these householders were similarly designed for comfort as well as display. We may imagine the juvenile Chaucer in an undergarment of woollen cloth surmounted by a loose woollen tunic that hung down to his ankles.

It is not possible at this late date completely to re-create the atmosphere of Chaucer's family home. In his poetry mothers are celebrated as tender emissaries of a largely patriarchal society; they are patient and benign, meek and gentle. It would be unwise, however, to interpret his life in terms of his art. The women of his poetry also tend to be deserted and betrayed, for example, although there is no evidence that Agnes de Copton experienced any such fate. It has also been observed that 'father figures' in Chaucer's poetry are noticeable by their absence but, again, no proper conclusions can be drawn.

His father did intervene in Chaucer's life in one decisive period, however. In 1347, as part of his official duties as deputy butler in the king's household, he was despatched with his family to Southampton in order to supervise the collection of import duties upon wine; the year after the Chaucers left London the city was visited by 'the death', later named the 'Black Death' after the black buboes which swelled upon the victim's body. It has been estimated that 30 per cent of the English population was destroyed by the epidemic of 1348–9. In the unnaturally crowded and noisome conditions of London we may suppose the mortality to have been significantly higher, but no reliable estimates are extant. It is safe to assume, however, that when the Chaucer family returned to Thames Street in late 1349 or early 1350, they found a much emptier city. The effect upon the young Chaucer can only be inferred. The only reference to a plague epidemic occurs in 'The Pardoner's Tale':

> Ther cam a privee theef men clepeth Deeth
> That in this contree al the peple sleeth.

But it is merely an elaboration within an ironic moral homily on the sin of avarice.

It is suggestive that Boccaccio's *Decameron*, which may have influenced the design of *The Canterbury Tales*, was conceived as a series of stories designed to alleviate the pressing miseries of the plague. It has been supposed that Chaucer's well-attested absorption in books springs directly from his experience of a threatening and uncertain reality; that he was possessed by the idea of reading as the image of a secure world. There may be some truth in this but it would be unwise to project a modern sensibility upon a medieval mind. The citizens of fourteenth-century London, in particular, were inured to death and disease in all of its forms; it should be remembered, too, that for them death was only one stage of an eternal drama. The consequences of the plague epidemic were for the Chaucer family considerably more benign, in any case, since they inherited a great deal of property from the last bequests of those relatives who had unfortunately remained in London.

On his return to the city it might be assumed that Chaucer's schooling began in earnest, except that there is no indication of what that schooling consisted. The education of a prominent citizen's son characteristically began at the age of seven in a 'song school' or 'grammar school' where Latin phrases were learned by rote; Geoffrey Chaucer might equally have been taught at home, or even by the priest of St Martin Vintry. Many scholars have acquiesced in the notion that he was sent to St Paul's Almonry School, just a short walk away, if only to explain how the poet acquired his knowledge of Latin and of Latin authors such as Ovid and Virgil. Here he would have learned the Latin grammar of Donatus, known to generations of schoolboys as the 'Donat', as well as more advanced rhetorical and grammatical treatises; here, too, the Latin was as likely to be translated into French as into English, an indication that the Anglo-Norman ascendancy had not wholly faded. All this is supposition and speculation, however, compounded by the nervous belief that Chaucer's genius must have in part depended upon a formal and hierarchical education. The problem is that no evidence can be furnished to support that belief. One possible source of instruction, however, lies closer to home. A written compendium of English texts, assembled by a London bookshop around 1330, has become known as the 'Auchinleck Manuscript'; it contained more than fifty items, including seventeen English romances as well as saints' lives and satires, and has been credibly associated with the Chaucer household itself. Certainly some similar anthology would have been known to the young Chaucer. Like Shakespeare Chaucer nurtured his genius by absorption and assimilation; his early exposure to English texts would, in that sense, have been highly significant. His was a thoroughly native genius.

Chapter Two
A Courtly Training

Chaucer's formative education took place in the royal household. His name is first announced to the world in the accounts of Elizabeth, Countess of Ulster, in May 1357, when 'ii s' were given to 'Galfrido Chaucer Londonie'; in the same period the young Chaucer was given a 'paltok' or short doublet suitable for a page in royal service. Princess Elizabeth was married to Prince Lionel, second son of Edward III, king of England; this is an indication that the Chaucers of London commanded enough influence and respect at court to place their son in an enviable position.

His life as a young page was peripatetic, travelling with the royal household from Windsor to Woodstock, Hatfield to Anglesey. The constant movement from castle to castle, estate to estate, was only increased when the household of Princess Elizabeth was merged with that of her husband in the autumn of 1359. Chaucer was now, nominally at least, a page in the service of Prince Lionel of Ulster. It was an education and a career, a profession and a duty. In his study of English law, composed in the fifteenth century, Sir John Fortescue claimed that the royal court furnished 'schooling in athletics, moral integrity and good manners'; it was indeed a nursery in all the arts. The young Chaucer would have been provided with lodging and appropriate clothing, like the paltok mentioned in the household accounts, but his family would have been responsible for any other expenditure. It was money spent well, however, since their son would have grown up among the most noble and notable of his contemporaries; he was beginning to climb upon a gradually rising hierarchy which led to the summit of royal administration and good governance. There would have been a clerk or priest of the household who acted as *pedagogus* to the pages and taught them grammar and languages. In time, also, he would have been taught how to read, and to write, official documents; it is clear from his later service that he was instructed in all the arts of diplomacy. The courteous or 'gentle' man, for example, must be 'well-seyinge' and 'full of wordes'. It might almost be the definition of a poet.

In these early years, however, he would have been an attendant and servant. There were instruction manuals which expounded the arts of civilised behaviour to the young page while waiting upon his elders and betters, with precepts such as 'be careful where you spit, and keep your hand before your mouth . . . you must only hold the meat with three fingers of your left hand when you cut it. That is courtesy . . . do not bite your bread but break it.' The young Chaucer would also have been instructed in the arts of conversation, conducted in French or in Latin; he would have been taught, too, the basic elements of music, which would have included dancing and singing. In the *Household Book* of Edward IV, one of the duties of young squires lies 'in pipeing or harpeing, synginges, or other actes marcealls, to help to occupy the court, and accompanie estraingers'. The young

Squire, in *The Canterbury Tales*, sings and plays the flute:

> Syngynge he was, or floytynge, al the day . . .
> He koude songes make and wel endite.

It has often been supposed that Chaucer did indeed compose court songs on the themes of love and chivalry;
nothing in his early education would disprove the idea.
There can be no doubt, too, that he would have been
acquainted with the chivalric romances which played so
large a role in court entertainment; the evidence of his
poetry suggests that he had a natural ear for cadence and for
rhyme, and the difference between English and French verse
would not have been lost upon him. The world of fable and
of chivalric adventure was one of spectacle and of display, of
ritual and formal measure; it may have encouraged a sense
of magnificence and power but, in a sensitive and intelligent
boy, it might also induce a sense of irony and of drama. The
distinction between life and art was one that he himself
would draw in his own poetry.

The young page was discouraged from playing dice or
hazard, but there were games of more reputable pedigree to
while away the vacant hours. All the activities of hawking
and hunting were central to court life; hunting in particular
encouraged a form of ritualised violence which well
corresponded with the chivalric ideal. Chaucer introduced
the pursuit into one of his earliest long poems, *The Book of
the Duchess*, and his use of technical terms revealed that he
was thoroughly familiar with it. At this late date hunting
may be dismissed as an anachronistic and even barbaric
sport, but in Chaucer's lifetime (and far beyond) it was

central to the idea of a civilised society: a measure of the distance we must travel in order to understand Chaucer and his world. It was an aspect of the chivalry that he extolled in his portrait of the Knight in *The Canterbury Tales*, and indeed in 'The Knight's Tale' which follows the 'General Prologue' of that poem.

The practice of chivalry was not necessarily romantic,

English soldiers besiege a French town

however. The next reference to Chaucer in the royal
accounts concerns his capture on the field of battle. He was
in the company of Prince Lionel, despatched to France in
order to further the plans of his father, Edward III, to be
crowned king of France in Reims; it was a small company,
part of a larger force led by Lionel's brother, John of
Gaunt, the king's third son, and its role in any fighting was
correspondingly small. Chaucer and his military companions may have been present at the siege of Reims, and
may have taken part in the sporadic skirmishes in the
vicinity. His observations of siege warfare there may
emerge in some lines from *The House of Fame*, where he
recalls 'the roaring' of the stone when it is loosed from its
catapult:

> . . . .the rowtynge of the ston
> That from th'engyn ys leten gon.

His company eventually made its way to the town of Réthel,
twenty miles north-east of Reims, and by mischance
Chaucer was captured in the neighbourhood by French
forces at some time in the middle of November 1359. A
chronicler has given a general account of how several
knights and squires 'were killed at night in their quarters,
and . . . foraging parties taken in the fields'. It is likely that
Chaucer was a member of one such foraging party, looking
for desperately needed food and other supplies in the rain
and winter landscape of hostile France.

He was ransomed, four months later, for the sum of
sixteen pounds – an appropriate sum for a *valettus*, or
yeoman, which Chaucer may now be deemed to have

become. The poet never mentioned the incident in his later verse, unlike his French contemporaries who often engaged in autobiographical sallies. In *The House of Fame,* however, there is also a reference to the 'pelet out of gonne', and in the same poem there is an allusion to music played on trumpet, horn and bugle in order to excite feats of military ardour:

> Of hem that maken blody soun
> In trumpe, beme, and claryoun;
> For in fight and blod-shedynge
> Ys used gladly clarionynge.

Whether this comes from memory, or imagination, is an open question. There is an account of warfare in 'The Knight's Tale' which is couched in the alliterative form of Old English, as if his own memories were conflated with childhood reading of the English romances. Thus he describes how, 'Ther shyveren shaftes upon sheeldes thikke'. Chaucer is often considered to be a 'bookish' writer, and the poet himself went to some trouble to present himself in a similar light; it is as if he fled from his own experience into the realms of art. Indeed the image of the agreeable and diplomatic Chaucer seems somehow out of place in the context of murderous hostilities. It is known, however, that he returned to France seven months later in order to accompany Prince Lionel during the negotiations for a treaty; he was also considered reputable and responsible enough to take certain personal letters from his employer back to England. But nothing more is known about his experience of warfare. He emerges in this period as a recognisable, if junior, member of the royal household. A respectable and successful career lay before him.

The events of Chaucer's life remain unrecorded for some years after the campaign in France of 1359 and 1360. In 1361 Prince Lionel was despatched to his Irish fiefdom as viceroy, but there is no evidence that the young page travelled with him. It is likely that he remained in England, therefore, but his duties and employments from 1360 until 1367 remain unknown. A similar period of Shakespeare's early life has also receded from view, this happy coincidence of 'lost years' reminding biographers that no one can ever be wholly understood.

It has been conjectured that Chaucer entered the household of John of Gaunt at this time; certainly Gaunt became his principal patron in later years, and awarded him a life annuity for his services. It has also been surmised that, on the departure of Lionel to Ireland, the young page entered the household of the king, Edward III, himself; an official document of June 1367 names 'Geffrey Chaucer' as a yeoman in that household, '*noster vallectus*' or our valet, but this may imply that he had only recently assumed the post. From that time forward, in fact, he was customarily noted as one of the sovereign's *familia,* and was generally travelling under the protection of the king.

There is a third possibility, and one more intriguing since it takes him out of the immediate context of court service. One of Chaucer's sixteenth-century biographers and editors, Thomas Speght, believed that Chaucer had been enrolled for the study of law at the Inner Temple in London and that 'manye yeres since, master Buckley did see a

recorde in the same howse, where Geffrye Chaucer was
fined two shillinges for beatinge a Fransiscane Fryer in
fletestreate'. The supposition that Chaucer studied law may
be dismissed as a further example of the wishful thinking of
those who believe that a great and in some sense learned
writer must have benefited from a formal education such as
they themselves had once received. It seems not to occur to
them that genius is genius precisely because it flourishes in
the most unlikely conditions; as John Dickens said of his
illustrious son, 'he may be said to have educated himself,
sir'.

Yet there are stray indications that Speght's testimony is
not wholly unreliable. Buckley was indeed keeper of the
records at the Inner Temple; the offence and the fine, for
which Chaucer is noted, were also apt and appropriate for the
period. The standard wisdom of Speght's contemporaries
was that Chaucer had attended either Oxford or Cambridge
universities, and that in any case the Inner Temple did not
receive pupils; so his information was surprising as well as
enlightening. That is no guarantee of its veracity, of course.
Buckley may have wanted to attach 'the father of English
literature' to his institution, and did not care by what means
this was accomplished. The offence of beating a Franciscan
may also have been deemed highly appropriate for a poet
who was often considered to be a proto-Protestant. The
evidence, then, is ambiguous. Common sense and clerical
expediency, however, would suggest that there must have
been some training at the Temple in the fourteenth century.
The mastery of law was protracted and difficult; it is recorded
that, in 1381, books belonging to 'prentices of the law' were
burned in the street by a disaffected mob. In later years a

legal education was considered to be a necessary preliminary
to a career in royal and even ecclesiastical service. The young
Thomas More, in many ways an apt image of his great
predecessor both as a London writer and as a royal servant,
was instructed at one of the Inns of Chancery.

There is indeed the incontrovertible fact that Chaucer was
trained, or somehow trained himself, in all the arts of
rhetoric. There can be no doubt that his poetry is
established upon the rules and constraints of the rhetorical
tradition, as it had been bequeathed in handbooks such as
Geoffrey of Vinsauf's *Poetria Nova*. Chaucer knew all the
procedures of repetition and personification, amplification
and digression. There is indeed a hint of his attachment to
the legal Inns in his description of a 'gentil MAUNCIPLE was
ther of a temple':

> Of maistres hadde he mo than thries ten,
> That weren of lawe expert and curious.

It has been argued in recent years that much of the verse and
drama of England emerge indirectly from the legal debates
of the Inns where, under the guise of 'Put the case that . . .',
fictional narratives were created for the delectation of a
judicial audience. The earliest plays were performed in the
halls of the various legal Inns, and masters of prose such as
More acquired their skills in the little theatres of the 'moot'
and the courtroom. In that sense Chaucer's supposed
sojourn in the Inner Temple would set an historical and
literary precedent. But it cannot be proved. It can only be
concluded that Chaucer employed technical terms used in
legal discourse, and was very well acquainted with the

procedures of judicial dispute such as 'herbergage' (lodging):

> 'Ha! ha!' quod he, 'For Cristes passion,
> This millere hadde a sharp conclusion
> Upon his argument of herbergage!'

Any residence at the Inner Temple would also help the biographer to explain Chaucer's acquaintance with the other great poet of this period, John Gower, who had himself been a member of the same institution. Gower seems to have embarked upon a legal career, and by his own account wore '*la raye mancé*', the striped robe of the sergeant-at-law; he was a little older than Chaucer, and had already acquired a reputation as a writer of French poetry, but they were well enough acquainted for Chaucer to name him as his lawyer when he was despatched on royal business overseas. Theirs was, perhaps, a marriage of minds.

Chapter Three
The Diplomat

When Chaucer next appears in the historical record, in 1366, he is already in the king's diplomatic service. In February of that year a warrant for his safe conduct was issued by the king of Navarre, in the name of '*Geffroy de Chauserre escuier englois en sa compaignie trois compaignons*'. The nature of this mission by Chaucer and three unnamed companions is not certainly known. It has been suggested that they were travelling to Spain on pilgrimage to the shrine of St James of Compostella, where they might wear the pilgrim badge of the scallop shell, but this is unlikely. Folk longed to go on pilgrimages, but not in the Lenten season. It is far more probable that they were engaged on a secret mission concerning the affairs of Pedro of Castile; he had aligned himself with Edward III's oldest son, known familiarly as the 'Black Prince', but was facing an imminent invasion from France. Whether Chaucer was engaged in negotiations with the king of Navarre, or whether he was persuading certain English forces to assist Pedro, is unknown; it is only important to note that at the age of twenty-four he was being entrusted with important and perhaps clandestine diplomatic business. He was a rising member of the royal household, and would move upwards ineluctably through the ranks of *valettus* and esquire: a 'new man', coming from the world of London merchants and businessmen and financiers, who was also able to position himself within a more ancient and honourable hierarchy of the realm. Yet his position was therefore ambiguous; he was deemed to be one of the gentility, but he was not of aristocratic rank. It might be suggested that as a result he was in the best possible position to observe, and to understand, the social changes and displacements taking place all around him. Some of the Canterbury tales concern these 'new men', and the pilgrims debate the conflicting claims of noble birth or personal virtue as the guarantors of 'gentillesse'. It was an abiding preoccupation of Chaucer's generation.

There were other ways of acquiring royal patronage. Chaucer's father died in the early months of 1366 and, although his will is not extant, it is inconceivable that his only son was not left some part of a large estate. With the advantage of inherited wealth and property Chaucer found himself conveniently placed to marry Philippa de Roet, herself already a lady in the household of Edward III's consort, Philippa. In the household accounts there is reference to 'Philippe Pan', which has been construed as 'Paon'; Philippa would then be the daughter of Sir Paon de Roet.

The marriage of Geoffrey Chaucer and Philippa de Roet was no doubt what a future generation would call a 'career marriage'. It was by no means unusual for members of the royal household to unite themselves even more closely in this manner, in emulation of their employers, and we may see Chaucer's social life following the established routines of the fourteenth-century court.

In the early autumn of that year 'Philippe Chaucer' was

A lady of the chamber helps her mistress dress her hair

granted a life annuity of ten marks by Edward III and described as '*une des damoiselles de la chambre nostre treschere compaigne la roine*'; as one of the ladies of Queen Philippa's chamber, she may have been able to further her new husband's career and reputation.

Very little is known of the Chaucers' domestic and familial life. There seems to have been a first-born daughter, Elizabeth Chaucer, who was admitted to the Black Nuns in Bishopsgate Street in 1381 and who later entered Barking Abbey; she disappears into mysterious seclusion. More is known about Thomas Chaucer. He was born in 1367 and at an early age entered the household of John of Gaunt; he remained in courtly service all his life, and rose through the ranks to become a very rich and thoroughly successful man. His daughter – Chaucer's granddaughter – finally resolved the distinction between the merchant class and the aristocracy by becoming duchess of Suffolk. The lifelong quest of the Chaucers for 'gentle' status was finally achieved.

John of Gaunt also interested himself in the affairs of Elizabeth Chaucer, since it was he who paid for her admission to the Black Nuns, a payment that has led some Chaucerian biographers to fear the worst. It has been inferred that both Thomas and Elizabeth were in fact the children of Gaunt by Philippa Chaucer, and that the poet was used willingly or unwillingly to confer legitimacy upon them. It is certainly true that Philippa's sister, Katherine Swynford, later became John of Gaunt's official mistress; but any other relationship exists only in the area of speculation. If true, it would immeasurably deepen and complicate Chaucer's relationship to the social and courtly world; it would also throw an interesting light upon his characteristic irony and

Pencil design for 'Chaucer at the Court of Edward III'. Ford Madox Brown's nineteenth-century vision of the poet at court

detachment. But at this late date nothing is known or can be proven. To all appearances Geoffrey and Philippa Chaucer have all the attributes of a 'professional couple' working in harmony, and such an arrangement need not necessarily be at the expense of love, trust and affection.

Even as he was acquiring a reputation as a skilled negotiator, Chaucer had already made his mark as a skilful poet of the court. By his own account he wrote 'many a song and many a leccherous lay'. It is likely that these earliest verses were composed in French for a predominantly French-speaking court; we may imagine the young Chaucer reciting them to a small audience like that portrayed in his *Troilus and Criseyde*, where three ladies are sitting 'withinne a paved parlour' listening to a 'geste' or verse story. Indeed a manuscript of contemporaneous French love poems survives, with the notation of 'Ch' against fifteen of them. They are sufficiently melodious and inventive for a young and aspiring poet and, if they are indeed by Chaucer, they serve to emphasise that his early work was firmly set upon the model of fashionable French poetry.

The court of Edward III was in many respects itself dominated by French custom. His wife, Philippa, came from Hainault; his mother, Isabella, had been a French princess. The captured king of France had been living in England as a willing or unwilling hostage, and continued all the arts of patronage while in captivity. The verses of Machaut and Froissart, Deschamps and Graunson, were widely circulated; Chaucer met Froissart after the French poet had joined the household of Queen Philippa, and there is some evidence of mutual influence. There is a further connection, which bears testimony to the variously interlinked groups which comprised late medieval society. Philippa Chaucer's father, Paon de Roet, was a knight of Hainault. From the same principality came Queen Philippa,

Philippa of Hainault, Edward III's French queen. Chaucer's wife, also called Philippa, served in her household

as we have seen, and Froissart himself. There was, in other words, a Hainault affinity to which Chaucer had an intimate attachment.

So at the beginning of his poetic career Chaucer wrote complaints and roundelays, ballades and envoys, on the themes of love and passion. It was a literature of longing, established by the rules of courtly etiquette and by the laws of *fine amour* or what in *The Legend of Good Women* Chaucer termed 'the craft of fyn lovynge'. His contemporary, John Gower, records that 'in the floure of his youthe' Chaucer filled the whole land with ditties and with glad songs, some of which still miraculously survive in his collected works. Much of Chaucer's court poetry has disappeared, as the natural result of time and inattentiveness, but poems such as 'The Complaint unto Pity' and 'A Complaint to His Lady' testify both to what has been called the natural music of Chaucer's verse and to his mastery of poetic diction. In his early years, too, he was an inventor and an experimenter. He introduced the rime-royal stanza and *terza rima* into English verse; he was the first to employ the French ballad form, but he changed the French octosyllabic measure into what has become characteristically English decasyllabics:

> O verry light of eyen that ben blinde,
> O verrey lust of labour and distresse . . .

He invented the native measure.

Yet there is one achievement that surpasses all of his technical skills. After his first forays into French court verse he chose to write in English for a predominantly courtly audience. He had enough confidence in his own skills, and in his own language, to adopt a native muse. In that sense he can be said to anticipate the rise of English in the fourteenth century. His was a period when the status of the native language was being elevated, and its usage becoming much more widely and securely based; in Chaucer's lifetime it replaced French as the language of school-teaching. The Anglo-French language, derived from the Norman conquerors, had long dominated social discourse. But the court of Richard II was the first, since the time of the Anglo-Saxons, in which English was the principal language. Everything conspired to render Chaucer the most representative, as well as the most accomplished, poet of his time.

When he began his career as a poet of the court there were obvious examples of English poetry all around him, from the romances of Sir Orfeo and Sir Launfal to the versified manuals and histories of various monkish chroniclers; there was also a fine lyric tradition, both secular and sacred. But there was no tradition of sophisticated courtly poetry in English; Chaucer adapted or assimilated the vocabulary and structure of fashionable French poetry, and effortlessly reproduced them within English diction and cadence. It is a significant achievement for a young poet, and did not go unremarked.

In fact one of his French models, Eustache Deschamps, sent Chaucer a 'ballade' a few years later in which he praised him as a 'grand translateur'. He was referring in particular to Chaucer's translation of *Roman de la rose*, a French allegorical epic on the theme of love. As Chaucer explains in some early lines:

> It is the Romance of the Rose,
> In which al the art of love I close.

The first section of some four thousand lines was written by Guillaume de Lorris in the early thirteenth century, and it was concluded half a century later by Jean de Meun, a scholar whose narrative of love is embellished by digressions and asides on a thousand different subjects. Chaucer chose to translate only passages written by the earlier poet. It is not clear whether he published his results to the world, but there are unmistakable signs of his ready wit and invention. We can almost see him marshalling his native language into appropriate shape:

> Though we mermaydens clepe hem here
> In English, as is oure usaunce,
> Men clepe hem sereyns in Fraunce.

He also evinces a genuine pleasure in the sensitive calibration between the Romance and Saxon elements of native speech:

> Largesse, that settith al hir entente
> For to be honourable and free.
> Of Alexandres kyn was she.
> Hir most joye was, ywys,
> When that she yaf and seide, 'Have this.'

It can be concluded that Chaucer, even at such an early stage in his poetic life, was possessed by the delights of diversity and variation; he constantly modified his poetic language to accomplish a wide range of effects, and was always intent upon changes of local detail. His tapestries of flowers, and his symphonies of birds, are rich and particular; he loved the art of miniature. When this is combined with vivid theatricality, and the sonority of the high style, then a most complex poetry may be created.

His *Romaunt of the Rose* is also the first indication that, by the act and art of translation, Chaucer reinvigorated the English language; when later poets celebrated his 'eloquence' they were describing his happy ability to incorporate the swelling measures of French and Italian poetry within his own style. Part of Chaucer's genius lay in translation; we may imagine a poet delighted by the art of the book. By his own account he found half of his experience in reading. What could be more natural for him than to meditate upon a text and slowly to reproduce it within the fabric of his own language?

In this context it may also be possible to begin to understand Chaucer's somewhat recessive temperament. His literary persona, manifest throughout his writings, is one of embarrassed bookishness; this is often considered to be a pose or device, quite at odds with his successful and prosperous career in the world, but there may be real truth within it. Why would he wish to create it in the first place, if it did not correspond with some powerful persuasion of his own? He chooses to hide behind words. Or, rather, he allows his personality to be dissolved within them. It can be said, for example, that as a translator someone is doing the writing for him. He does not have to claim authority or responsibility for what he is doing. This is of course precisely the tactic which he uses in his poetry; he shifts the blame, if that is the right word, upon his characters in *The Canterbury Tales*:

> For Goddes love, demeth nat that I seye
> Of yvel entente, but for I moot reherce
> Hir tales alle, be they bettre or werse . . .
> Blameth nat me if that ye chese amys.

He fakes an original source for his *Troilus and Criseyde*. 'Blameth nat me', he intercedes. 'For as myn auctor seyde, so sey I.' It is also the demeanour of the diplomat, presenting his case on behalf of a higher authority. The rhetorical procedures of his verse are in that sense characteristic; they become a device whereby he can conceal himself, ironically or otherwise. Rhetoric informs the texture of his narrative; it does the writing for him. He uses rhetoric so successfully, in fact, that he can detach himself from his poem. And was he also able to detach himself from his public career? Upon the stage of the world, where everyone played a part, it was important to become an accomplished actor.

In June 1367 Chaucer was awarded a life annuity of twenty marks (£13 6s 8d) by Edward III; since he is variously entitled '*valettus*' and '*esquier*' in the royal accounts, his rank must remain uncertain. In succeeding years he was also presented with gifts of winter and summer robes, as well as robes of mourning, appropriate to his degree. He was certainly considered valuable enough to be sent on various missions overseas. In the summer of 1368 he was given a licence to 'pass' at Dover; it has been suggested that he was travelling to Milan, where Prince Lionel (after the death of his first wife) had just been married to Princess Violante Visconti. He would then have been exposed to the cult of 'Franceys Petrak, the lauriat poete', Petrarch then being resident in the city, but the circumstances of his journey are not definitely known.

It is clear, however, that in the following year he travelled to France in the retinue of John of Gaunt as part of 'the voyage of war'. His role in these intermittent and fruitless hostilities, known to posterity as 'the Hundred Years' War', is not recorded. He did receive, however, a 'prest' or payment of ten pounds for services rendered. Yet the association with John of Gaunt is a significant one, attested by the annual grant he was soon to receive from him. John of Gaunt had become duke of Lancaster seven years before, after his marriage with Blanche of Lancaster. Edward III began his slide into credulous old age after the death of his wife in 1369, and as a result Gaunt's palace at the Savoy became the true centre of court life in England; his powers of patronage were now such that all sought his favour. Another event brought Chaucer closer to Gaunt's sphere of influence. In 1368, soon after his wedding to Princess Violante Visconti, Prince Lionel died; the rule of the ageing Edward III was increasingly uncertain, and Chaucer had need of new patrons.

He had left, as it were, a calling card. John of Gaunt's wife, Blanche of Lancaster, died of the plague in the autumn of 1369 – at the time when Gaunt himself was still engaged in his 'voyage of war' – but on his return to England he instituted a memorial service to be held each year for her in St Paul's Cathedral. Some historians believe that she died the year before, in 1368, turning Gaunt's expedition into a campaign of sorrowful forgetfulness as much as military hostility; but the nature of Chaucer's response remains the same. He composed a poem of consolation, entitled *The Book of the Duchess*, which elegantly and prettily extols Blanche's virtues while at the same time preserving her memory in the freely flowing poetry itself:

> Therto she hadde the moste grace
> To have stedefast perseveraunce
> And esy, atempre governaunce
> That ever I knew or wyste yit,
> So pure suffraunt was hir wyt.

The tone and diction of the poem claim it for oral delivery and it seems likely that *The Book of the Duchess* was first recited at one of the memorial services held in the cathedral; it is couched in a respectful but informal tone, as if the poet were on easy if not necessarily familiar terms with Gaunt himself. The work of a court poet in his mid-twenties, whose abilities were already widely recognised, it is presented in the form of a dream vision, a form highly congenial to Chaucer's imagination which always works by indirection and ambiguity; in dreams there are no responsibilities. When dealing with 'high' matters, such as the grief of the duke of Lancaster, discretion was advisable.

The poem itself belongs to the French tradition of *dits amoureux*, and in particular to Machaut's *Jugement dou Roy de Behaingne*. Its opening lines are, in addition, modelled upon the beginning of Froissart's *Paradys d'Amours*. Throughout Chaucer's poetic output, in fact, there will be found wholesale borrowings and appropriations. Half of his work derives from older and earlier sources. Yet we must forget modern notions of plagiarism and parody. One of the guarantees of virtue and sincerity, in a medieval text, lay in the fact that it derived from a greater authority. There was no merit in originality as such, only in the reformulation and refashioning of older truths. Yet *The Book of the Duchess* is no mere copy of *Paradys d'Amours*, or of any other of the texts to which it has been compared. The dry beat of Froissart's verse has become lush and melodious; the prolixity of Machaut's narrative style has been curtailed. The French preference for delicate rhetorical effects, and the lively expression of sentiment, has been excised in favour of narrative event and plain dialogue. The French sources have been absorbed, in other words, and out of them an English amalgam is created. It is the paradox of Chaucer's work: the materials are familiar but their expression is novel and surprising. As he said himself, out of old fields comes all the new corn.

Chapter Four
An Italian Connection

In the summer of 1370 Chaucer was given letters of protection by the king in order to travel '*ad partes transmarinas*'; these letters of protection were designed to protect the king's envoy from any legal suits that might be raised against him while he was out of England, a necessary precaution in such a litigious age, but they do not specify the nature of Chaucer's destination. It has generally been assumed, however, that he was sailing to Genoa; there were trade negotiations with that city during the same period. He had known Italian merchants all his life, and was fully acquainted with the business of wharves and imports. What could be more natural than that he should be sent on a trade mission to the busy port of Genoa?

It can be assumed that he knew the Italian language, also, since over the next few years he was sent on successive missions to Genoa and to Florence. In 1372 he was granted a warrant to negotiate with the Genoese for the construction of a special seaport in England for the merchants of that city. In that year too, he is first styled in the household accounts as '*armigero regis*', or esquire of the household, which suggests a corresponding degree of importance. It is not probable that he was also esquire of the chamber, part of the king's *secreta familia* which travelled with the monarch everywhere; he was more likely to be known for his skill in diplomatic missions, and retained accordingly. The journey to Genoa, for example, had other more secret purposes. He set out in December 1372, with two high-ranking Genoese together with servants and bodyguards. He had been given an allowance of one hundred marks – £16 13s 4d – and he was out of the country for some five months. It was his first extended trip to Italy, and it would affect him profoundly.

It would not be a safe or comfortable journey in the middle of winter, especially as the route of the English party took them over the Alps. We may imagine them with horses and baggage on mountain ways which, although customarily used by travellers, were none the less icy and vertiginous; their faces were muffled in scarves, their shoes bound up in cloth, as they struggled against the snow and wind. A contemporary of Chaucer, Adam of Usk, described how on an Alpine journey he was 'drawn in an ox-wagon half dead with cold, and my eyes blindfolded lest I should see the dangers of the pass'.

Genoa itself was the centre of a great trading empire, with a population approximately that of London in the same period. It was built of stone rather than of wood, however, and anyone who walks through the city's 'Old Town' will still be able to acquire some sense of how it seemed in Chaucer's lifetime – the narrow winding streets, the small churches, the statues of the Virgin on every corner, the workshops, the street-stalls. The negotiations must have passed successfully enough, since trade between London and Genoa materially increased in the years after Chaucer's embassy, but it seems likely that Chaucer had also been despatched to the city in order to hire Genoese mercenaries for Edward's campaigns against the French. The records for that more clandestine trade have of course not survived.

His mission to Florence was no less delicate, since he was sent there in order to facilitate previous negotiations concerning the king's loans from the banking family of the Bardi. Since Edward III had defaulted on his debts to the same family almost thirty years before, these negotiations could not have been without their local difficulties; but, once again, Chaucer seems to have been successful. He was

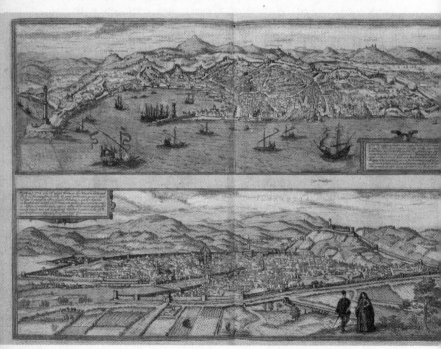

Sixteenth-century map of Genoa and Florence

awarded significant gifts on his return to England, in any event, and the journey to Italy consolidated his standing at the English court.

But his travels had more profound, if less visible, consequences. For three months he had experienced the society and culture of Italy; in particular he had been introduced to the wealth of Florentine cultural life by the rich banking families of that city whose libraries and art collections far surpassed anything that a London merchant would possess. It was the time of Florentine 'humanism', although of course the word itself would have meant nothing to Chaucer or his contemporaries. It would be indeed ill-advised to suggest that the English poet was somehow transformed overnight into a representative of the 'new learning', or that a glimpse of Giotto's art rendered him suddenly susceptible to the claims of 'realism' in artistic production. Certain biographers have suggested that he met Boccaccio and Petrarch on this journey, but this is also unlikely. What would he have said to them if he had met them?

He was residing in a city, however, which had become the nurse and mother of contemporary Italian poetry. It had three favourite sons, each of whom would have a powerful and permanent effect upon Chaucer's own poetic sensibility. They were, in chronological as well as literary order, Dante, Petrarch and Boccaccio.

Dante was of course the most significant Italian poet of the fourteenth century. His *Divina Commedia* was composed in the vernacular; he had written his epic of heaven and hell in letters of fire and had instantly given the Italian language pre-eminent status among all the tongues of

Europe. In addition he had written a defence of his decision in a formidably erudite volume entitled *De Vulgari Eloquentia*. This work 'concerning vernacular eloquence' had been written in the first decade of the fourteenth century, in precisely the period he had set to work upon the *Divina Commedia*. By the time of Chaucer's visit to Florence, almost seventy years later, it may have occurred to him that the English language might be capable of a similar transformation. His journey to that city may then have materially strengthened his resolve to write in English, and to render that language the medium of great art. It is certainly true that the poems Chaucer wrote, immediately following his journey to Italy, are heavily influenced by Dante's example. His next major poem, *The House of Fame*, is in fact almost a parody or pastiche of the Italian poet's grand manner.

In the period of Chaucer's travels Petrarch was living a hundred miles away from Florence in Padua; but the reputation of the greatest living Italian poet was everywhere apparent. Petrarch was the poet of magnificence who had almost single-handedly raised the status of the poetic maker into the company of kings. He had indeed been crowned with the laurel in the Roman senate, and was also variously proclaimed 'master' in the courts of Naples and of Venice. King Robert of Naples had presented him with an opulently embroidered robe of honour. No such awards and honours were available in England – nor ever would they be – but the elevation of Petrarch must certainly have encouraged Chaucer to see his poetic career as a vocation more than an employment. It is unlikely that, without the combined example of Petrarch and Dante, he would have considered the composition of such longer poems as *Troilus and Criseyde* and *The Canterbury Tales*.

These two poems also owe much of their inspiration to the third member of the Italian poetic trinity, Giovanni Boccaccio. Chaucer's love epic set in Troy, *Troilus and Criseyde*, borrows much from Boccaccio's *Il Filostrato*; it has been plausibly argued that *The Canterbury Tales* takes as its model the peripatetic story-telling of Boccaccio's *Decameron*. Chaucer never once mentions Boccaccio. By instinct, perhaps, he knew that the Italian poet was too close a source and inspiration to be confessed to the world. It is in fact easy to outline passages from Boccaccio which Chaucer transposed to his own work, but his principal influence was of a different kind. Chaucer discovered in the Italian poet the possible range and variety of poetic concerns – the epic story-telling of the *Decameron*, the classical mythology of *Ninfale fiesolano*, the narrative of Theseus entitled *Il Teseida*, the Trojan romance entitled *Il Filostrato*, and the Latin text 'on the genealogy of the Gentile Gods' *De Genealogiis Deorum Gentilium*. At the time of Chaucer's visit to Florence Boccaccio was also completing *De Casibus Virorum Illustrium*, a section of which the English poet lifted for one of his Canterbury tales. It is of more than passing interest, too, that Boccaccio was about to give a series of public lectures on Petrarch in Florence itself.

So Chaucer returned to England significantly changed by his experience in Italy. It has sometimes been supposed that he brought back with him certain manuscripts, particularly that of Dante's *Divina Commedia*, as gifts from the rich Italian banking families with whom he negotiated; given the

circumstances of fourteenth-century hospitality, this is likely
to be the case. We can certainly see the consequences of his
close reading, in the poetry he was soon to compose, but in
the meantime the life of the world kept on breaking
through. A few months after his return from his successful
mission to Italy, in August 1373, he was despatched to
Dartmouth in order to mediate between a Genoese ship-
owner and the port authorities there. John de Nigris owned
a vessel which for unknown causes had been placed '*sub
aresto*' by the men of Dartmouth; Chaucer was sent to
expedite its return to its owner, in which he was successful.
Once more Chaucer's connection with the Italian merchants becomes clear, as does his evident skill in difficult
negotiations. It is perhaps no more than coincidental that,
in *The Canterbury Tales*, Chaucer's Shipman 'was of
Dertemouthe'; the allusion is amusing, however, and opens
the possibility that some of Chaucer's invented characters
were based directly or indirectly upon 'real' people. He
would probably have denied any outright identification with
any of his contemporaries, but he may have divined in
certain people the outlines of idealised types.

Chaucer's evident success in these negotiations, and in
many others which have gone unrecorded, was rewarded
with various grants and annuities. In the spring of 1374
Edward III bestowed upon him the gift of a daily pitcher of
wine, a pitcher in this instance meaning a gallon-sized jug or
lagena, which Chaucer continued to receive until the day of
the king's death. Two months later he also received an
annuity of ten pounds from John of Gaunt, who had just
returned from further forays and incursions in France. It is
sometimes assumed that these favours were shown to him as

One of the Canterbury pilgrims, the Shipman, came from
Dartmouth, scene of one of Chaucer's diplomatic missions

a means of literary patronage, but this is most unlikely; if they were given for his oratorical skills, they were the ones he used as a diplomat and household messenger rather than as poet.

Chapter Five
The Civil Servant

The most important of Chaucer's royal posts was awarded to him on 8 June 1374 when, in his early thirties, he was appointed as controller of the wool custom and wool subsidy for an annual income of ten pounds per year with a bonus of ten marks. In this role he administered the collection of the various taxes and imposts paid upon exports of wool and leather leaving the Port of London; a sack of wool equivalent to 364 pounds in weight, for example, would be taxed at fifty shillings. At the same time he was made controller of the 'petty custom'. The 'petty custom' comprised taxes other than those imposed on wool; the goods included wax, cloth, beds, and what was known as 'divers merchandise'. It was not an easy sinecure, as some have suggested, but a responsible and in certain respects arduous job. Chaucer would have been responsible for keeping a 'counter-roll' of accounts to check those presented by the collectors of the tax. This 'counter-roll' had to be written in the controller's own hand, although none has survived from the pen of Chaucer himself. Since there was much scope for corruption, when ready money or 'bonds' were involved, Chaucer would have required a keen eye and a ready wit to authenticate what may have been somewhat dubious accounting practices. The accounts themselves were written in Latin, with an admixture of

French and English; it is an indication of the polyglot tendencies of the age, of which Chaucer took full advantage in his poetry.

The collectors themselves were responsible for investigating and weighing merchandise, counting the sacks of wool, settling disputes between merchants and the officials of the custom house, imposing fines and collecting custom duty. Chaucer himself may not have engaged in these activities, but he would need to be well acquainted with them. It was he who took action, for example, against merchants who had unlawfully landed cargoes upon the shore. He also retained control of a seal, or 'cocket', which was used to verify the legality of a shipment of wool or leather. In his oath he pledged to serve the king loyally, to remain on constant duty in the port of London '*en proper persone ou par suffisante depute*', and to render faithfully the custom accounts '*saunz fauxme or fraude*', without falsehood or fraud. That this was not some stock or standard injunction was made plain in the case of Richard Lyons, a rich London vintner and lifelong companion of Chaucer's father. In this period he was in overall charge of the petty custom and subsidy and thus Chaucer's employer; it is fair to assume, in fact, that he had some role in obtaining the post for his former friend's only son. But Lyons was an old-fashioned speculator who was not averse to pocketing money for himself; only two years after Chaucer's appointment, Lyons was accused of extortion, removed from his post, and despatched to prison. It cannot be said, then, that Chaucer had taken on an altogether comfortable appointment. In the beginning, at least, he seems to have dispensed with the services of a '*suffisante depute*' and, as custom required, to have filled out the rolls and accounts in his own hand.

It is of course a matter of historical regret that none of these hand-written accounts survives; a graphologist might then have found some inkling to Chaucer's character in this busy period. Here was a poet who, having acquired his reputation as a courtly poet of dream vision, now found himself surrounded by London businessmen and clerks who were hard-headed, argumentative and not averse to sharp practice. He had of course known these people all his life, and it can be assumed he had already evolved a way of conversing and of dealing with them. We may imagine a man of infinite bonhomie and tact, but shrewd and quick-witted none the less. He may even have prided himself upon his ability to move between two worlds – between the court and the city, between the poetry of love and the prose of business. It might almost be said that the variety and heterogeneity of his own verses lie precisely in their ability to live 'between' various poetic dispensations. He was a man of infinite jest.

In his next long poem, written after taking on the controllership, *The House of Fame*, his working life is peremptorily described:

> For when thy labour doon al ys,
> And hast mad alle thy rekenynges,
> In stede of reste and newe thynges
> Thou goost hom to thy hous anoon,
> And, also domb as any stoon,
> Thou sittest at another book
> Tyl fully daswed ys thy look.

We know of Chaucer's bookishness but, by good fortune, we also know precisely where his 'hous' was situated. The poet lived above Aldgate, one of the eastern gates of the city. The dwelling seems to have come with the job. The lease was granted to him a month before he took up the post of controller and it comprised, according to the *London Letter Book* of the period, 'the whole dwelling-house above Aldgate Gate [supra portam de Algate] with the chambers thereon built and a certain cellar beneath the said gate, on the eastern side thereof, together with all its appurtenances, for the lifetime of the said Geoffrey'. The property was also granted to him rent-free for the course of his life which, even by medieval standards, was a significant gift. His beneficent donors were the mayor, Adam de Bury, together with the aldermen and the '*communitas civitatis Londonie*'; but it seems like the civic authorities were acting at the behest of, or in collaboration with, the royal court. The bonds and affiliations between the courtiers and the richer merchants were, as we shall see, very close indeed.

The property itself was spacious enough for a rising official. It comprised the floor above the gateway itself, including the two towers on either side and a large rectangular room between them. The towers were some twenty-six feet across and twelve feet in depth (nearly eight metres by over three-and-a-half metres), while the intervening room was some twenty feet by twelve (six metres by over three-and-a-half). There were two smaller rooms behind the towers. The 'hous' was reached by spiral stone stairways on either side; there were two windows, one looking west into the city and one east towards the suburbs beneath the wall and to the country beyond; Chaucer also had access to the parapet running along the wall itself. It was named 'Aldgate' or 'Aeldgate' because of its antiquity stretching back, in the medieval phrase, beyond the memory of man; in the thirteenth century it was repaired after various armed incursions into the city had rendered it 'ruinous'. In

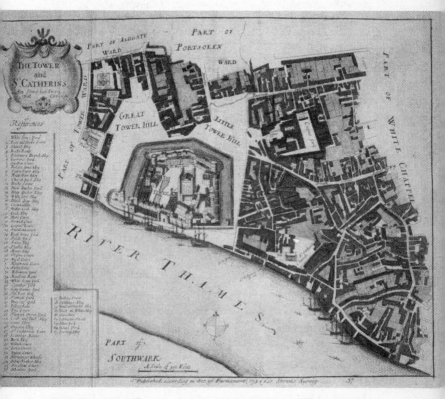

Engraving for *Stow's Survey of London* published in 1754. Aldgate, where Chaucer lived in chambers above the gateway itself, was on the east side of the city

the words of the antiquary, John Stow, it was 'repaired, or rather newly built, after manner of the Normans, strongly arched with bulwarks of stone from Caen in Normandy, and small brick, called Flanders tile'. The topography of the area has been well described, by Stow and others; it comprised the usual London mingling of gardens and workshops, grand houses built of squared stone and sagging low-roofed tenements, inns and hostels for travellers together with wooden sheds and stalls, yards and alleys, stables for horses and churches for the faithful.

The noise of the city began at dawn when the porter of Aldgate, William Duerhirst, opened the gates. It was the signal for the commercial life of London to begin, with the entry of innumerable pack-horses, carts, wagons and traders on foot bearing eggs and poultry from the suburban farms. A toll was levied on each horse or vehicle, in order to pay for the road leading to Aldgate itself. Chaucer woke each morning to the sound of the traffic below, and it would have been the constant accompaniment to all the work he undertook in his lofty apartment; he would have discerned, too, the various cries of entry and departure in the endless passage of people and of goods. He would have recognised certain voices, like that of the porter William, as well as the distinctive call of each trade or profession. But of course the gate was also erected as a means of defence. In times of civic tension chains and bars were attached to the gates, and guards assigned to their positions on the walls; at the time of the insurrection later known as the 'Peasants' Revolt' Aldgate itself was covertly opened by an alderman, William Tonge, to allow the rebels access into the city. It says something about Chaucer's proximity to major urban events that he was residing above the gate at the time. What sounds would he have heard then?

From the eastern window, looking out towards Essex, Chaucer would have known the sprawling and squalid suburb which had grown up beside the wall. Here were cheap lodgings, inns, cook-shops and stalls selling supplies for the vast army of travellers who made their way in both directions. Chaucer describes such a place with its 'hernes' (hiding places) in 'The Canon's Yeoman's Prologue':

> 'In the suburbes of a toun,' quod he,
> 'Lurkynge in hernes and in lanes blynde,
> Whereas thise robbours and thise theves by kynde
> Holden hir pryvee fereful residence . . .'

From the window in the west he would have looked out over the city itself. Just within the city bounds, a few yards from Chaucer's lodging, was the famous meeting-place of 'Aldgate Well' with its water-bearers carrying their leather buckets. The manor house and gardens belonging to the earl of Northumberland were in the immediate vicinity, together with the church of St Katherine Coleman and the manor of Blanche Appleton where basket-makers and wire-drawers had their shops. The priory of the Holy Trinity was also here. Some of the houses adjoining that priory, which Chaucer would have known, were excavated in Stow's time; by the sixteenth century they were already 'two fathoms deep' under the soil, comprising 'a wall of stone, with a gate arched of stone, and gates of timber to be closed in the midst towards the street'. The poet would have passed these gates almost every day. It is an indication of how quickly

London was built and rebuilt, even within Chaucer's own lifetime, and how new buildings were erected on the ruins of the old. It was a place of perpetual change. From Aldgate to his work in the Port of London he would have walked through the busiest, noisiest and most populous streets of the city. From his vantage above the gate he was well acquainted with the figure of the traveller and with the image of life as an endless journey.

He lived here for twelve years, during which period he wrote *The House of Fame* and *The Parliament of Fowls*, 'The Knight's Tale' and *Troilus and Criseyde* from which this local reference to driving the beasts in or having to stay ('bleven') outside is taken:

> The warden of the yates gan to calle
> The folk which that withoute the yates were,
> And bad hem dryven in hire bestes alle,
> Or all the nyght they moste bleven there.

It is sometimes assumed that his was a domestic as well as a creative environment, and that with his wife, Philippa, he lived in familial contentment above the thriving city. This was in fact not the case. They were a professional couple who generally lived apart. Their mutual supporting role is emphasised by the grant of ten pounds each year which Chaucer received from John of Gaunt, since the annuity was also awarded 'for the good service that our well loved Philippa, his wife, did for our honoured lady and mother the queen, whom God pardon, and for our very beloved companion the Queen [of Castile]'.

Here lies a story. Soon after the death of Blanche, commemorated by Chaucer in *The Book of the Duchess*, John of Gaunt married Princess Constanza of Castile. Philippa Chaucer seems to have become a member of the Gaunt household upon the death of Queen Philippa; after this second marriage she became a 'damoiselle' in attendance upon Constanza, and in 1372 had been granted an annuity of ten pounds. Over the next few years she also received money and gifts from John of Gaunt. She was more than a paid attendant, however. Her sister, Katherine Swynford, had become John of Gaunt's mistress and had an important place in the household. So even while Philippa Chaucer was in attendance upon Constanza, her sister was an attendant in quite another sense. That Philippa and Katherine were very close is not in doubt: when Katherine eventually set up her own household in Lincolnshire, Philippa and her son, Thomas Chaucer, followed her. It throws an interesting light upon the nature of the royal household, where ties of loyalty and affinity were intertwined. The suggestion that Philippa herself had a liaison with Gaunt, and that her children were part of that union, and not Geoffrey Chaucer's children, has already been raised. Whatever the truth of that matter, it is clear that personal religious faith or public professions of morality had nothing to do with the court which Chaucer inhabited. When reference is made to the poet's irony and scepticism, in all human affairs, his immediate circumstances might usefully be taken into account.

He was, in every sense, deeply implicated in the world around him. In the summer of 1375 he stood as 'mainprise' or security for John de Romsey, the treasurer of Calais who had once been Chaucer's superior in the royal household; it seems that he was accused over the seizure of the goods belonging to a man accused of sedition. In effect Chaucer made himself legally responsible for the appearance of Romsey before the Court of the Exchequer. It could not have been an onerous or perilous responsibility, since Romsey was treasurer of an important English possession, but it illuminates the network of duties, favours and obligations that comprised the social life of the period. In later years he would act as surety for other old friends, with the unspoken assumption that they would perform the same service for him.

There were other and more profitable services that Chaucer could undertake. In the same year as he stood mainprise for Romsey, he purchased the 'wardship' of two Kentish heirs. This was a highly profitable venture whereby orphaned heirs of the king's tenants, if they had not come of age, were given into the protection of suitable guardians who managed their estates for them. Chaucer purchased the right to look after the affairs of Edmund Staplegate, the son and heir of a wealthy Canterbury merchant, which two years later he relinquished to him for the sum of £104. Staplegate had bought back 'his marriage and the custody of his lands', so we can assume that Chaucer would have had some role in arranging a suitably profitable union for the young heir. It may seem odd that a stranger might purchase control of your life for a significant period, but it was an ingrained part of medieval social law. Staplegate himself was murdered twelve years later, in another example of that constant interplay between intricate legalism and explosive violence.

Chaucer must in fact have considered himself affluent in this period since, the month after buying the wardship of Edmund Staplegate, he also purchased the guardianship of William Soles; Soles was heir to the manors of Betteshanger and of Soles in Kent, and may again have seemed like a rich prize in the medieval battle of life. The fact that both heirs came from Kent is significant, in the sense that in later years Chaucer himself would be heavily identified with Kent both as Member of Parliament and as Justice of the Peace. He lived in that county after leaving London, where it is surmised that he wrote much of *The Canterbury Tales*, and it is at least possible that he already owned property there at this early date.

His affluence in this period, then, is not in doubt – well-paid employment, a wife in well-remunerated royal service, a free house leased to him for the rest of his life. There is no extant record of his silver or of his tapestries, of his beds and 'tables' or paintings, but he makes one reference to his possessions in the prologue to *The Legend of Good Women*:

> Yis, God wot, sixty bokes olde and newe
> Hast thow thyself, alle ful of storyes grete.

Of course a line in a poem could not be taken as evidence in a court of law, but the specific allusion to 'sixty' books – he could have written 'twenty' or 'thirty', and maintained the cadence – does at least suggest the presence of individual memory. He might be accused of boastfulness, however, since to possess sixty books was to possess wealth and luxury. But the fortune accruing to these books was, for

Chaucer, of quite a different kind. As he also wrote in *The Legend of Good Women*:

> And yf that olde bokes were aweye,
> Yloren were of remembraunce the key.

Books were for him a source of doctrine and of delight; they were the very source of knowledge and tradition, without which nothing could certainly be understood. Chaucer lived upon books; he adapted books; he translated books; he copied books endlessly in his own writing; he understood, too, that by the alchemy of his writing, old things were made new, as familiar and ever renewed as the daisies with which in *The Legend of Good Women* he contrasts the art of reading itself. Art and nature are not severally divided in his work; they are aspects of the same abiding reality which is endlessly re-created:

> For out of olde feldes, as men seyth,
> Cometh al this newe corn from yer to yere.

By his own account Chaucer possessed a 'cheste' for some of his volumes. Books were considered so valuable, in fact, that in libraries they were chained to the shelves and could only be loaned on the security of a significant deposit. But we may also imagine Chaucer in the fortunate position of the clerk in 'The Miller's Tale' who possessed:

> His Almageste, and bookes grete and smale . . .
> On shelves couched at his beddes heed.

The paradox is of course that most of the prepared manuscripts of Chaucer's own poetry were manufactured after his death; the paucity of evidence for manuscript circulation in his own lifetime suggests also that most of his poetry was conveyed by oral delivery.

Chaucer had a well-paid governmental position, but it was not necessarily a secure one. In the last years of Edward III's reign there were continual complaints of nepotism and maladministration, largely brought about by the king's lax hold upon affairs of state. There were favourites who suborned the commonwealth, officials who engaged in full-scale bribery, and courtiers who used their influence corruptly. It is the usual story of a reign coming to an end. Yet it might have affected Chaucer directly. In the 'Good Parliament' of 1376 the Commons, under the leadership of its first elected 'Speaker', Peter de la Mare, delivered their main grievance in the complaint that the king 'has with him certain councillors, and servants who are not loyal or profitable to him or the kingdom'. Among the miscreants named were Alice Perrers and Richard Lyons, both of whom were closely associated with Chaucer himself. Lyons was specifically accused of using his position as 'farmer' of the petty custom in order to extort money. Chaucer's friends were under attack. Perrers was banished from the household, and Lyons was incarcerated for an indefinite period. It would seem likely, then, that Chaucer would be caught in the general rout of corrupt officialdom. He was, after all, Richard Lyons's deputy and friend. Yet he survived.

He was perhaps not considered prominent enough to be mentioned in the Commons' indictment. The Members of the Parliament House were pursuing the principal figures in what they considered to be a malign conspiracy; to have brought in Chaucer, and other of his contemporaries, would have deflected their main accusations and weakened their case. It is also possible that as a result of the king's incapacity the principal man in the realm, John of Gaunt, threw the shield of his favour over one of his chosen men. He was certainly powerful enough to be able to overturn the decisions of the Parliament House later that year, and to imprison or otherwise remove from office the leaders of the 'Good Parliament'. Peter de la Mare, for example, was arrested and imprisoned. Nevertheless it must have been a salutary warning to Chaucer, and a reminder that the favour of princes might not be wholly benign.

Yet he was still deeply involved in royal business. In the last week of December 1376 he was despatched upon a clandestine mission on the king's behalf – '*in secretis negociis domini regis*' – but the nature and purpose of the mission are unknown. He may have been concerned with the imprisonment of Peter de la Mare in Nottingham Castle. He may have been engaged in negotiations for the marriage of the young heir apparent, Richard, with a princess of France. The latter seems most likely since he was accompanied by the brother of Richard's tutor. Yet nothing is certain. All that can be said with some authority is that Chaucer was personally involved in the most pressing matters of the realm. He was not a poet who happened to be a diplomat and government official; he was a government official and diplomat who, in his spare time, happened to write poetry.

Over the next few months, in fact, he embarked upon no less than four separate missions to France. He was so occupied that in the spring of 1377 he was given leave to

appoint a deputy to his post at the Port of London, Thomas
Evesham, on the grounds that '*sepius in obsequio nostro in
partibus remotis occupatus*'; he was, in other words,
occupied on the king's allegiance in distant lands. The
purpose of these journeys is again obscure – his first
destination was Paris, but the others are not recorded – but
the likely concern is once more with the proposed union of
the young Richard with the French dynasty. And the matter
was no longer hypothetical. On 21 June 1377, at the palace
of Sheen, in the words of Froissart, 'The gallant and noble
King Edward III departed this life to the deep distress of the
whole realm of England'. All was changed.

Chapter Six
The Court of the Boy King

The change of reign, however, did not affect Chaucer directly. Richard II, the young king, was grandson of Edward III and son of the 'Black Prince' who had died in 1376. He was only eleven years of age when he succeeded to the throne of England and, throughout his minority, John of Gaunt was largely responsible for the conduct of the realm. Gaunt was never proclaimed as regent but he was none the less the 'steward' of England. Chaucer might at least feel secure in his role as controller of the wool custom; the day after the death of the old king, Edward III, he was reappointed to the post. This may have been an entirely formal undertaking, given the transference of royal power, but it may none the less have been reassuring. Chaucer's own family were also likely to benefit from Gaunt's ascendancy. His wife and son were part of Gaunt's household; in particular, his sister-in-law, Katherine Swynford, was in a position of unusual influence as Gaunt's mistress.

Chaucer was also well acquainted with the members and supporters of the young king's household; he knew the chamberlain, Robert de Vere, and the sub-chamberlain, Simon de Burley, who at various times expedited the progress of Chaucer's career. He knew the rich merchants of the city who subsidised the king, among them Nicholas

Brembre and John Hende. He knew the Ricardian 'knights of the chamber' such as John Clanvowe, Richard Stury, Lewis Clifford, William Neville and Philip la Vache; to the latter Chaucer addressed one of his most interesting short poems, entitled 'Truth'. These friends and acquaintances emerge through Chaucer's public life in the customary and familiar role of witnesses or guarantors. Most of these Ricardian knights had in fact been attached to the old king's household in the period when Chaucer had also been enrolled there as an esquire; he had grown up in their company. He was very well connected, in other words, and perfectly equipped to weather the storms of factional politics which disturbed the realm in subsequent years.

But the knights also had a more intimate association with Chaucer. Lewis Clifford had brought back for Chaucer's delectation the poem which Eustache Deschamps had composed in the English poet's honour; it was the verse in which he celebrated Chaucer's role as the 'great translator' of French culture. John Clanvowe was an author; he wrote poetry, and an unpublished religious treatise entitled 'The Two Ways'. They must have made up part of the audience to which Chaucer addressed his own poetry.

There is one other matter which touches upon Chaucer's concentric circles of friendship and affinity. Many of the knights to whom he was socially or informally attached are suspected of being religious reformers; from the evidence of contemporary chronicles, wills and scattered historical allusions it is evident that they had some sympathy with the Wycliffites or lollards who were intent upon purging the Church of its worldly excesses. It need not be inferred that these knights were radical reformers, who denied the doctrine of transubstantiation or who rejected the sacrament of confession; they were, rather, intelligent and sophisticated men who deplored the corruption of the Christian faith. It ought to be remembered, too, that John of Gaunt protected Wycliff in his confrontations with the ecclesiastical authorities. There was a network of rich and powerful courtiers who were explicitly opposed to the arrogation of power and wealth by the prelates of the Church.

There is no real reason to doubt that Chaucer was sympathetic to their aims. On the face of it he was a man of unexceptionable piety. In one picture he is depicted with a set of rosary beads in his hands (see jacket image). One of his early poems, entitled *An ABC* and described in the manuscripts as 'La priere de Nostre Dame', is an elaborate encomium on the blessed virtues of the Virgin Mary; it is, however, a close translation of a French poem and may have been composed as a form of verse experiment. That is not to

John Wycliff, whose followers became known as the lollards

doubt its sincerity: a poem to the Blessed Mother was a token of public respect (or, perhaps, respectability) and might also merit good marks in the struggle for private salvation. He also composed a life of St Cecilia, which later saw service as 'The Second Nun's Tale' in *The Canterbury Tales*, but it is imbued with supernaturalism rather than piety, and in that sense resembles an old-fashioned '*geste*'.

The Canterbury Tales itself bears witness to Chaucer's piety in another sense. It is well known that it ends with 'The Parson's Tale', a penitential sermon which itself concludes with Chaucer's retraction. He disavows all of those poems 'that sownen into synne', which include many of the Canterbury tales as well as *Troilus and Criseyde*, and recommends only that literature which 'is writen for oure doctrine'. These may be the conventional sentiments of a medieval author preparing himself for death, but they may also afford a glimpse of Chaucer's genuine faith. A large proportion of *The Canterbury Tales* are overtly Christian in theme and inspiration, while ecclesiastical protagonists figure prominently among the roll-call of pilgrims. It is here that the question of lollardy arises, since in the framework of *The Canterbury Tales* Chaucer obliquely or indirectly satirises all the representatives of the Church's hierarchy. The Prioress is silly and self-indulgent; the Summoner is grotesque and corrupt; the Pardoner is an effeminate hypocrite; the Monk is worldly and greedy; the Friar is, in Chaucer's own words, 'a wantowne and a merye'. Only the Parson fulfils God's commandments and he, significantly, is suspected by the Host of being a lollard. Chaucer seems to be intimating here that the calls for religious reform should be heeded, if the purity and grace of the Church are to be re-established upon earth. Of course he never makes such statements directly; all the forces of his nature and character prompted him into modest disclaimers of personal opinion. Unlike his contemporary, William Langland, he never broke out in passionate remonstrance. But the general sentiment is clear enough. He joined forces with his knightly colleagues in desiring a wholesale reform of Church practices. This is not to claim him as a lollard or a Wycliffite, however. There is no evidence that he wished to undermine the sacramental system, or cast into doubt the rituals, of the Church. It should be remembered in this context that the lollards opposed pilgrimages, particularly to that saint whom they nominated as 'Thomas of Cankerbury'; it would have been odd, to say the least, to devote a long poem to just such a pilgrimage. Instead Chaucer seems to have shared the opinions of the most intelligent men of his period.

The accession of the new king did not materially affect Chaucer's employment as a diplomat. In the spring of 1378, for example, he was sent on a mission to Lombardy concerning '*lexploit de notre guerre*' – the conduct of our war. The war in question was of course that against France which, on the death of Edward III, had been inflamed by several French incursions against the Channel ports. The English counter-offensive had begun inconclusively in the year of Chaucer's mission and, by the time of his departure, was effectively stalled. Chaucer was travelling to Lombardy in order to find allies. He had with him a retinue of six officials and bodyguards; his English superior in the negotiations, Sir Edward de Berkeley, had about twice that number. They had come to treat of war and money. They paid suit particularly to Barnabo Visconti, the lord of Milan, and the English mercenary commander, Sir John Hawkwood. Chaucer's was to be a protracted mission of some five months; he arranged for a deputy to take his position in the controllership of the wool custom and also appointed his friend and fellow poet, John Gower, as his attorney ready to conduct legal business on his behalf. It seems possible that, even at this early stage, there was the prospect of a legal challenge of '*raptus*' or rape by one Cecily Champain. We may be allowed to envisage a man who was under the pressure of some heavy private anxieties.

It says much about Chaucer's emollient reputation, however, that he had been despatched to enter negotiations with a man who was generally perceived to be a cruel if single-minded tyrant. We have Chaucer's own word for it. In 'The Monk's Tale', Barnabo Visconti is apostrophised thus:

> Off Melan grete Barnabo Viscounte,
> God of delit and scourge of Lumbardye.

In *The Legend of Good Women* the God of Love is asked to treat his subject, Geoffrey Chaucer, mercifully

> And not ben lyk tyraunts of Lumbardye.

So Chaucer was entering Milan as if he were entering a tiger's den. The mercenary, Sir John Hawkwood, was also Visconti's son-in-law. Power and violence were compounded in this northern city, therefore, and Chaucer was considered the man to deal with them in every sense.

There was one other grave matter which had brought them to Italy. Pope Gregory XI had died on 27 March 1378, two months before Chaucer's departure. A conclave of cardinals had elected Pope Urban VI, amid scenes of mob violence and intimidation; the Roman crowds demanded a Roman, or at least an Italian, pope after the enforced reign of the popes in Avignon. The cardinals, supposed to be in secret conclave, were in fact threatened by the mob that pillaged the Vatican in the process. But sharp beginnings often have unfortunate ends, as Chaucer himself once had cause to notice, and the pontificate of Urban VI was already proving to be disastrous by the time Chaucer had reached Milan. It was said that his sudden elevation had disturbed his mind; he railed against his cardinals, and had to be physically prevented from attacking one of them. When the bishops came to pay homage to him in Rome, he accused them of deserting their flocks. When given money due to the Holy See he told his treasurer 'to keep thy money to thyself, to perish with thee'. It is almost as if a lollard had ascended the throne of Peter. In August of that year, when Chaucer was still in Milan, the cardinals fled from Rome and in the relatively safe kingdom of Naples declared that the election of Urban was invalid and in his place raised Clement VII to the pontificate. Thus began the Great Schism, which had incalculable effects upon the political and religious history of Europe for the next forty-five years.

Chaucer was at the centre of events at a time of huge instability. The election of two separate popes, with separate allegiances, threatened the power relations between all the nations of Europe. It was to be expected that Visconti of Milan would attach himself to the Italian

Pope, Urban, but in an age of internecine warfare and subtle stratagem no one's loyalty or fidelity could be taken for granted. Sir John Hawkwood also controlled the finest mercenary army in Europe, so that his decision on the matter could powerfully affect the course of events. We do not know how Chaucer conducted himself in this affair; we may imagine, however, that he employed skill and good humour.

There were other negotiations in Milan which subtly accompanied those of war and peace. The newly crowned king, Richard II, needed a suitable wife. It was now proposed that he should marry the daughter of Barnabo Visconti, Caterina, a union which promised wealth as well as military alliance to the English king. The fact that these negotiations proved eminently successful is exemplified by the two Milanese ambassadors who returned with Chaucer to England in the autumn of that year. They were bringing with them proposals for the marriage, as well as a very large dowry.

There were other treasures to be brought back from Milan. In the great hall of the palace there, where Chaucer would have first confronted Visconti, the frescoes of Giotto sent out their own light into the proceedings. Petrarch had been godfather to Barnabo Visconti's son, and Barnabo's court was known to hold literary pre-eminence throughout Italy; it was rivalled only by that of his brother, Galeazzo Visconti, who ruled in Pavia and who had been Petrarch's patron for many years. Like many tyrants, they combined violence with a love for the beautiful. In particular Barnabo Visconti's library was by general consent the greatest in the country. There were some four hundred volumes in place here; it was the treasure-house of Italian literature which included works by Petrarch and Boccaccio as well as Dante's *Divina Commedia*. It has in fact often been remarked that it was only after Chaucer's sojourn in Milan that his poetry seems thoroughly to have absorbed the influence of Boccaccio. He may have studied the manuscripts there, but his diplomatic business could not have allowed him the luxury of continual contemplation. It is far more likely that Visconti, in reward for Chaucer's excellent services as a diplomat and vicarious suitor for his daughter's hand, gave Chaucer several of the Italian poet's works. 'The Knight's Tale' is in places a close translation of Boccaccio's original, *Il Teseida*. The resemblances are so close and continuous that Chaucer could not have relied upon a free memory of earlier reading; he must have had the manuscripts to hand, and worked upon them line by line or stanza by stanza. Since he could not have found copies of the Italian books in London, or even in Paris, it seems most likely that he brought them back across Europe as gifts from Barnabo Visconti. So did an Italian tyrant alter the course of English literature.

The first product of this unlikely union is to be found in *The House of Fame*, a comic poem of some two thousand lines which ends abruptly and inconclusively with the phrase:

> 'But he semed for to be
> A man of gret auctorite . . . '

Indeed the whole notion of authority seems to be parodied in this poem concerned with unsteady fortune and false reputation. In his official services, Chaucer had come across many instances of fickleness or 'brittleness' in the affairs of the world, and this poem is in one sense conceived in playful mockery. It uses the old English octosyllabic metre which has over the centuries become the engine of English humour:

> Of trust, of drede, of jelousye,
> Of wit, of wynnynge, of folye.

It is the unembarrassed cadence of 'simple' English, often dedicated to the task of deflating pomposity or magnificence; it can also be used as an agent of self-deprecation, which is of course one of Chaucer's favourite devices.

The poem opens with a dream or, rather, with a disquisition upon the nature of dreams. It has generally been argued that Chaucer borrowed the device of the dream vision from the French poets, most notably from Guillaume de Lorris's *Roman de la rose,* but it is also worth noting that the dream is an essential part of the English imagination. Chaucer's contemporary, William Langland, established *The Vision of Piers Plowman* in a series of dreams. The first poem in English, by Caedmon, was heralded by a dream. The works of John Bunyan, and of Lewis Carroll, are striated with dreams. Chaucer is always part of an English, as well as a European, dispensation; that is the source of his strength.

'Of Decembre the tenthe day' Chaucer dreams that he is within a temple made of glass in which have been placed many curious statues and images. The story of the fall of Troy, and in particular the doomed love of Dido for Aeneas, are 'peynted on the wal'; it is the most famous love story in medieval Europe, and thus has pride of place in a temple dedicated to Venus. He wanders beyond its doors and finds himself in a wide desert, where he calls upon Christ to save him from phantoms and illusions. When he casts his eyes towards the heavens a more palpable reality presses down upon him in the shape of a giant eagle:

> Hyt was of gold, and shon so bryghte
> That never sawe men such a syghte,
> But yf the heven had ywonne
> Al newe of gold another sonne;
> So shone the egles fethers bryghte,
> And somwhat dounward gan hyt lyghte.

The bird might have flown out of Dante's *Purgatorio* where, in the ninth canto, an eagle '*con penne d'oro*' snatches the poet from a dolorous valley and carries him towards the sphere of fire. Passages such as this encouraged the fifteenth-century poet, John Lydgate, to declare him 'Dante in Inglissh'. Immediately after the appearance of the eagle, in fact, Chaucer addresses his audience:

> Now herkeneth every maner man
> That Englissh understonde kan.

There is no Dante in English. There could never be a Dante in English. Chaucer could no more copy Dante than he could fly in the 'pawes' of the famous bird. That is why the eagle is no far-sighted and prescient symbol of contemplation but, in *The House of Fame*, a garrulous and condescending bore whose voice seems to have been recognisable to Chaucer's audience. It might have been John

Gower, or Ralph Strode, or some member of the court. The truth is that Chaucer could not remain serious for very long; he could not maintain a 'high style' when his instinctive comedy keeps on breaking through. The eagle takes up the poet and in the course of their aerial journey he discourses upon the nature of sound, the composition of 'the Milky Wey' and the qualities of Chaucer's own poetry. It is a highly artificial and literary poem which makes fun of literariness and artifice. The nature of the English imagination eschews solemnity and parodies high-mindedness; it also allows Chaucer to parody his own endeavours and to present himself as an innocent and somewhat hamfisted celebrant of love's virtues:

> And peynest the to preyse hys art,
> Although thou haddest never part.

When the garrulous eagle eventually releases Chaucer, the poet finds himself beside a vast rock of ice on which are engraved the names of many famous men and women; some have melted away while others remain firmly etched, according to the position of the sun, and together they comprise a little homily on the adventitious nature of fame. Chaucer then encounters a castle of beryl, upon which have been placed the images of poets and musicians and storytellers. It may be construed in that sense as a castle of art, except for the fact that beside these illustrious images are those of 'magiciens' and 'jugelours'; art is then conflated with illusion and sorcery as another fickle source of fame. One of the magicians mentioned is 'Colle tregetour' –

> Y saugh him carien a wynd-melle
> Under a walsh-note shale.

This conjuror, who placed a windmill under a walnut shell, was in fact an Englishman known as 'Colin' who did indeed perform feats of magic; from the specificity of the reference, it seems likely that Chaucer witnessed one of his extraordinary performances. The reference to him here is part of the poet's habitual device of suddenly including real people within fictional surroundings; it is part of his wish, or ability, to destroy the illusion of art by appeals to the real world. Colin's trick of concealing a windmill beneath a nutshell may also be a token of the whole world contained within the brain or the imagination. It then becomes a very powerful image indeed, and helps to deepen the nature of the poem as a meditation upon the nature of poetry itself. It ought also to be emphasised, in this context, that poets are gathered in the castle through the existing fame of their stories rather than through any singular achievement of their own. Chaucer is thoroughly medieval in the sense that he does not consider the worth of the individual poet. From this, too, springs his own habitual irony and self-effacement.

Within the castle itself sits 'Our oune gentil lady Fame' who dispenses her favours to sundry petitioners with no sense of fairness or justice. There are those whose good deeds earn them unhappy reputations, while the renown of others is wholly lost. It is all a lottery and a japery. Chaucer understood the business of fame very well, and had stood at close quarters with many famous men; it seems likely, then, that his irony is in part fuelled by his observations of those all around him.

But there is another aspect of fame. It seems likely that *The House of Fame* was written after his return from Italy in 1378. The manifest influence of Dante can be cited in this respect but, more importantly, the cultures of Milan and Pavia were saturated with the notion of poetic 'fame'. It was one of the lodestones of Italian civilisation, propounded by Dante and celebrated by Petrarch. It is as if Chaucer were in fact satirising Italian predilections and propensities from a somewhat more sober or disillusioned perspective. When a member of the rout gathered around Lady Fame asks Chaucer if he, too, is there to acquire fame he replies firmly and forthrightly in the negative:

> For no such cause, by my hed!
> Sufficeth me, as I were ded,
> That no wight have my name in honde.
> I wot myself best how y stonde.

I have no wish to be blown about by the winds of fame; I know my situation best, and will never lose sight of it. In many ways *The House of Fame* is Chaucer's most auto-biographical poem in which he asserts his own stubbornly individualistic creed in the face of Italian or French aesthetic imperatives.

Yet of course it is at the same time concerned with the nature and status of poetry itself. If the dream vision was in fact a journey into his own imagination, as has been suggested, then the eagle is taking Chaucer into the furthest reaches of his own consciousness where the questions of poetry and fame are continually debated. In the palace of fame itself he sees pillars of various metals upon which are set the great writers of the past, each one bearing up the fame of his civilisation. Josephus holds up the fame of the Jews, Statius that of the Thebans, and Homer that of the Greeks. Is there any sense in which Chaucer believed himself capable of holding up the fame of the English? Yet in the same poem he apologises for the paucity of his style:

> Here art poetical be shewed,
> But for the rym ys lyght and lewed . . .

Out of this paradox, or inconsistency, springs laughter as well as contemplation. The comedy itself comes from embarrassment and self-deprecation, from the deliberate parody of the 'high style' together with the deflation of pomposity and wordiness. 'I do no diligence,' he writes in this poem, 'to shewe craft, but o sentence.' I am not concerned with literary devices but with substantial matter. It is the voice of the pragmatic and empirical temper, which has echoed through centuries of English prose as well as poetry.

It is sufficiently English, therefore, to take Chaucer as one of its first representatives. Much has been said concerning Chaucer as the 'father of English poetry', so much in fact that it has become something of a literary and cultural platitude; but Chaucer has become representative of so much else that, for writers such as G. K. Chesterton, he turns into the figure of England or the face of Albion. He is the genial and smiling emblem of Englishness – the man of practical affairs who turns his hand to poetry, the modest disclaimer of his own merits, the invisible man who leaves only the breath of good humour behind. Such a man, of course, is also known as William Shakespeare. It is the national icon.

The poem ends with a vision of the 'House of Daedalus', a great house of twigs which whirls continually about and from which issue all the false and true reports of the world. It is a box of Chinese whispers or, rather, a turning wicker cage 'of werres, of pes [peace], of mariages'. It is his own world of court and business gone awry, a mad vision of worldly affairs, in which the narrator himself seems lost and bewildered. There are many critics who have found in this poem evidence of Chaucer's own unhappiness or incapacity, at that time of his life when he was not sure in which direction his poetic vocation stood. He was a diplomat and official whose duties must have in some sense conflicted with, or curtailed, the practice of his art. He had returned from Italy with the manuscripts of Boccaccio, but he could have seen no way of emulating such prodigal and self-assured achievement.

His own success in the public world was fickle and unstable. He explicitly mentions 'Decembre the tenthe day' at the beginning of *The House of Fame*, as if it represented a specific occasion. Only a few lines later he refers to 'pilgrymage myles two' to 'Leonard'; only two miles from his chambers in Aldgate lay the convent of St Leonard at Stratford-le-Bow, from which Chaucer's Prioress would later emerge for her Canterbury pilgrimage. We may be equally specific about the date. On 10 December 1379, three representatives of the Vatican were recompensed and rewarded for their journey to England. They had come to expedite negotiations for the marriage of Richard II to the daughter of the Holy Roman Emperor, Anne of Bohemia.

The marriage with Caterina Visconti, over which Chaucer had spent many months of arduous business, had been abandoned for reasons of statecraft.

The vagaries of diplomatic life enter in indirect, as well as direct, ways. It has been concluded that the topography of *The House of Fame*, with its palace and its rock of ice and its giant house of twigs, is like some inverted dream version of the Ile de la Cité in Paris, with its Great Hall of pillars, its long gallery of glass and sculptures, its echoing bourse of merchants with their wooden stalls. From the roof of the long gallery there, hung the leg-bone and claw of a vulture. This was the area where, in 1377, Chaucer had gone to negotiate yet another of Richard's marital propositions. Everything comes together in this comic poem of fickle fate, inconclusiveness and disappointment. Yet, like the walnut shell, it also contains a greater world. In the house of twigs are found 'shipmen and pilgrimes' as well as 'pardoners'; the Shipman and the Pardoner make up two of the pilgrims whose subsequent journey rendered Chaucer immortal.

Chaucer, royal servant and diplomat, served three kings of England: Edward III, Richard II and Henry IV.
Above: Edward III with his son, Edward Prince of Wales (The Black Prince) who died in 1376. Edward III was succeeded in 1377 by his eleven-year-old grandson, Richard II, who was overthrown by Henry Bolingbroke (Henry IV) in 1399.

(*Above*) Pages serve John of Gaunt who is dining with the King of Portugal. As a young man, Chaucer worked as a page in the royal household. (*Below*) Chaucer was acquainted with court entertainment, so would have been familiar with fables of chivalry and romance.

John of Gaunt (*left*) was Chaucer's patron. Gaunt held power in England as 'steward' while Richard II was little more than a child. Chaucer's wife, Philippa, and his son, Thomas, were part of Gaunt's household, where Chaucer's sister-in-law, Katherine Swynford, was Gaunt's mistress and, later, wife.

Below: Coronation of the boy king, Richard II.

Chaucer was influenced by the Italian writers Boccaccio (*far left*), Petrarch (*left*) and Dante (*right*). Chaucer, in turn, influenced William Blake who in 1810 published his famous engraving, 'Sir Jeffery Chaucer and the Nine and Twenty Pilgrims on their Journey to Canterbury' (*below*).

caſcuno poſſ3 accuſarc denuntiarc 7 not
tēngnuto dc credença 7 aducit debia lotcr
condannatione Liquale ſe fēſſe 7 ſcodeſ
dc quella, cotale accuſa denuntiaxione 71

Above: Weighing wool.
In 1374 Chaucer was
appointed controller of
wool custom and wool
subsidy.
Left: The death from
plague of Anne of
Bohemia, queen of Richard II.

FACING PAGE:
Portraits of Chaucer:
Above left: From the poem
'Regement of the Princes'
by Thomas Hoccleve
(1368–1426).
Above right: From the
frontispiece of *Troilus and
Criseyde*: Chaucer reading
or reciting poetry to the
court. The king, Richard
II, is prominent in golden
robes. *Below*: From a page
of the fifteenth-century
Ellesmere Manuscript of
The Canterbury Tales.

Images from *The Canterbury Tales*:
the Monk and his greyhounds; the Cook; the Squire, the Friar.

Chapter Seven
A Nest of Troubles

It was difficult, even for a royal diplomat, to avoid the depredations of medieval law. In the autumn of 1379 Chaucer was obliged to hire a lawyer, Stephen Fall, to defend him before the King's Bench in a case of 'trespass and contempt'; the action against him had been brought by Thomas Stondon, but the identity of that plaintiff has been thoroughly obscured by time and circumstance. The nature of the case is also unclear, but the fact that it was to be heard before the King's Bench suggests that it was of some significance. Nothing further is known of the matter, however, and no doubt it was settled 'out of court'. This was a highly litigious age, and it has been estimated that in each law term there were more than 1,000 pleas or bills being conveyed through the various courts. No one as eminent as Chaucer could have avoided being caught in its machinations.

There was one case, however, which seems to have had more serious implications. On 1 May 1380, Cecily Champain – identified in the Chancery document as Cecilia Chaumpaigne – released Chaucer from all actions '*de raptu meo*', concerning my rape. It can be presumed that she, too, had settled 'out of court'.

The charge of '*raptus*' was a serious one which until the beginning of the fourteenth century had merited the

The Court of King's Bench, Westminster Hall

punishment of castration; by Chaucer's time, it had been commuted to one of simple hanging. It was also a rare offence, generally accounting for 2 per cent of all possible felonies. Its seriousness must have prompted Chaucer into bringing forward as witnesses for the document some of the most powerful men in the kingdom – among them Sir William Beauchamp, chamberlain of the king's household, Sir John Clanvowe and Sir William Nevill, two knights of the king's chamber and close associates of Chaucer, as well as his immediate superior as collector of the customs, John Philipot. Two years before, Philipot had been elected as lord mayor of London. This is testimony, strong enough to be used in any court of law, that Chaucer was very well connected indeed. He was not an amused observer of events from afar; he was at the heart of court and administrative affairs. And these men had now become Chaucer's representatives, prepared to testify on his behalf that there should be no prosecution. They were indeed eminently successful, since Cecily Champain did not press her case.

That indispensable collection of documents and materials relating to Chaucer, *Chaucer Life-Records*, prints three other documents which are relevant to Cecily Champain's 'release' of Chaucer. Two months later, in the court of the mayor and aldermen of London, Richard Goodchild and John Grove released Chaucer from any actions or suits at law; Goodchild was a cutlerer, and Grove an armourer, of London. They were prominent citizens of the merchant class, with whom Chaucer was of course very familiar. On the same day Cecily Champain released Goodchild and Grove from any similar suits or actions. Four days later, in the same London court, Grove recognised that he owed

Cecily Champain the not inconsiderable sum of ten pounds. It is all a very tangled web.

The medieval courts had proceeded no further with Chaucer's prosecution and, before we commit Chaucer to the sentence of posterity for rape, it might be as well to examine the evidence. Apologists for the poet have suggested that '*raptus*', in the official document, signalled not rape as such but some kind of forcible kidnapping which was not uncommon in the period. It would have been usual, in that instance, for a phrase such as '*abduxit*' or '*asportavit*' to be included with '*rapuit*'; no such addition was made. On the other hand if '*raptus*' meant in the modern sense rape – that is, forcible copulation and coerced sexual intercourse – then it was usual for words such as '*violavit*' or '*defloravit*' to be employed. There was also a phrase of the same import, '*afforciavit contra voluntatem*'. None of these words or phrases is included in the document. What, then, is the meaning of '*raptus*'?

The moral and social confusion is compounded by Chaucer's friendship with Alice Perrers, who, after the death of the queen, Philippa, had become official mistress to the king himself, Edward III. A powerful figure at court and in the city, Alice Perrers has generally been regarded by historians as an avaricious and unscrupulous female who alternately cajoled and compromised the ailing king. But she had at least one saving grace: she was closely acquainted with Geoffrey Chaucer.

For ten years she had been a lady of the queen's chamber. Philippa Chaucer, wife of the poet, also served in the queen's household. Alice Perrers was by marriage part of a prosperous London family. One of her closest friends, Richard Lyons, had been an intimate of Chaucer's father and happened to be Chaucer's immediate superior at the petty custom. She was also friendly with Adam de Bury, the mayor who had granted the lease of Aldgate to Chaucer. She owned much property in the vicinity of Aldgate. Wherever we look in the affairs of daily life we observe, in characteristic medieval fashion, a pattern of associations and affiliations.

On this occasion two of the figures in the pattern, their relationship now almost obscured by time and forgetfulness, are Geoffrey Chaucer and Alice Perrers. He was deeply compromised by the world in which he worked. And, as it happens, she was the step-mother of Cecily Champain. There are, as it were, wheels within wheels.

We can presume, then, that through his friendship with Alice Perrers Chaucer had a long acquaintance with Cecily Champain. He was in his late thirties; Cecily was, at the best calculation, in her very early twenties.

At this point presumption must end, and speculation take its place. Chaucer's wife, as a member of a distant and peripatetic court, was absent for much of the time; and the association between Chaucer and Cecily Champain may have led to a deeper and stronger relationship. If Cecily Champain believed that she was being neglected or otherwise misused – that she had in some sense been betrayed or compromised – there was open to her one legal remedy which would force Chaucer into acknowledging his direct role in her life. She could accuse him of '*raptus*' and then wait for him to negotiate a settlement with her.

The three later documents are of even more obscurity. It is possible that Cecily Champain found herself with child in the intervening months. This would have thrown an interesting legal light on the claim of *'raptus'*, since it was believed that no woman could conceive if she had not previously consented to intercourse. A payment of ten pounds might then have been considered suitable recompense. Any other theory must also be placed in the realm of speculation.

There may, however, have been a child. In a later production, entitled *A Treatise on the Astrolabe*, Chaucer addresses 'Lyte Lowys my sone' who has reached 'thy tendir age of ten yeer'; the text itself uses the year 1391 as the year for its complex astronomical and astrological calculations, and there is no reason to doubt that this was also the year of its composition. So little Lewis was born in 1381, just a few months after the legal complications with Cecily Champain. It is an intriguing if inconclusive story, and one which lends an interesting perspective to Chaucer's poetical claims that he was a stranger in the court of Venus and unskilled in the arts of love. He may have been more artful than the world has previously recognised. The truest poetry may be the most feigning.

It may also be the most plausible and significant way of dealing with public events. The negotiations for the marriage of Richard II and Anne of Bohemia were progressing but the daughter of the latest Holy Roman Emperor was also being pursued by Charles of France and Friedrich of Messien. In this period Chaucer wrote a poem about three competing marriage proposals, the difference being that his narrative concerns marital disputes among birds. It is a favourite medieval device – to offer a comic alternative world which acts as a commentary upon the human one. It is not necessarily conceived in a spirit of parody or satire, but rather of joy at the multifarious nature of creation.

The Parliament of Fowls opens in a familiar fashion; the narrator is absorbed in the reading of a book 'write with lettres olde', but he is so thoroughly tired that he retreats to his bed. There he dreams and is met in vision by a guide who leads him to the temple of Venus. This must have been so familiar to Chaucer's listeners or readers that it had become the equivalent of his private seal – a token of his personal style, albeit one conceived in a spirit of irony and self-mockery. Here once again Chaucer represents himself as a man who celebrates *fine amour* without in any sense having experienced it. As his guide puts it to him,

> For thow of love hast lost thy tast, I gesse,
> As sek man hath of swete and bytternesse.
> But natheles, although that thow be dul,
> Yit that thow canst not do, yit mayst thow se.
> For many a man that may nat stonde a pul
> Yet liketh hym at wrastlyng for to be . . .

It is the medieval equivalent of an old apothegm. Those that can, do; those that cannot, write. Since these lines were probably composed a little after the time of Cecily Champain's '*raptus*', about which everyone would have known, they contain more than a trace of irony. It is also somewhat ironic that this is the first poem in the English language which celebrates 'Seynt Valentynes day', and there is some justification for the argument that Chaucer initiated this festival in England in imitation of the Italian (and, specifically Genoese) holy day. It is one of his greatest, if least known, benefactions to the English. It is also likely that the poem was read at some kind of festive court ceremonial in honour of love's 'maistrie'; that would account for its relative brevity, and its general tone of intimate comedy relating to the rituals of love-longing and love-lament.

Despite the relative familiarity of Chaucer's theme, however, his means of expression have undergone a sea-change. The octosyllabic metre has given way to a more spacious decasyllabic, and the insistent beat of the couplet has been replaced by the more resplendent cadence of the rime royal based upon the Italian *ottava rima* which the English poet has appropriated from the works of Boccaccio. It provides a more plangent and commodious note:

> The lyf so short, the craft so long to lerne,
> Th'assay so hard, so sharp the conqueryng.

There has been nothing quite like it before in English poetry, at once majestic and easy, fluent and capacious. Chaucer was a great experimenter with poetic form. He introduced this rime royal into English literature, and as a result it was employed for three hundred years by poets who aspired to the 'high style'. We have also noticed how he fashioned the Dantesque *terza rima* into English shape, thus anticipating the 'experiments' of Thomas Wyatt by almost two centuries. It was a period when the language was at its most flexible and unpredictable; there were so many elements entering it for the first time that it was capable of the utmost change. It was rich and unfixed, altering with each generation of speakers. Chaucer, like Shakespeare, was stirred into life by a clamant and absorbent medium.

The rime royal of *The Parliament of Fowls* is a comprehensive form, also, since within it Chaucer can introduce the most blatant demotic:

> The goos, the cokkow, and the doke also
> So cryede, 'Kek kek!' 'Kokkow!' 'Quek quek!!' hye . . .

The plot of the poem is a simple one. Chaucer is introduced into the temple of love, and wanders into a glade close by where the birds of the earth meet on each Valentine's day to choose their respective mates. The formel or female eagle is pursued by three suitors, a royal eagle and two tersel or male eagles; they make their speeches of fidelity and truth, which are succeeded by the rude clamours of the lowlier birds tired of the protracted ritual. 'Have don, and let us wende! . . . Com of! . . . Al this nys not worth a flye!' The female eagle then asks for a year in which to consider her position, to which inconclusive judgement Dame Nature accedes. The poem ends with a roundel in praise of summer:

> Now welcome, somer, with thy sonne softe,
> That has thes wintres wedres overshake,
> And driven away the longe nyghtes blake!

The narrator takes his leave, and returns to the reading of his old books. Thus a public matter, of the king's marriage suit, becomes the occasion for a humorous and charming poetic diversion.

The Parliament of Fowls is also significant in terms of Chaucer's own poetic development. It has already been suggested that his metre is established upon the *ottava rima* of Boccaccio, and indeed the description of the temple in the poem is similarly derived from passages in the Italian poet's *Il Teseida*. If it had not been for Chaucer's encounter with the manuscripts of Boccaccio's work in Milan, the English poem would not have been written. There are other resemblances between the two poets. Boccaccio was the natural son of a minor Italian banker, and the bank's connection with King Robert of Naples eased the young man's entrance into the Angevin court there at the age of fifteen. In the same trajectory as that of Chaucer, he went from the professional urban class towards the nobility. Boccaccio soon found his poetic vocation at the Neapolitan court, and became a professional story-teller or entertainer for an audience of sophisticated courtiers. He composed dream visions and romances concerned with *fine amour*; more importantly, he composed them in the vernacular. The affinities, then, become clear. Even though neither poet could have observed it at the time, Chaucer and Boccaccio were part of a broad movement of taste and feeling.

It is all the more significant, therefore, that Boccaccio was the one writer with whom Chaucer set himself up in unacknowledged competition. Or would it be better to say that he entered into a dialogue with him, so that he might test the strength of his own English verse? He reduced Boccaccio's tendency towards libertinism, and generally moderated the excesses of the Italian poet's style. He shortened the sentiment and concentrated upon event and character; he introduced a prevailing ironic humour and engineered deliberate changes of mood and tone so that the tragedy and comedy were thoroughly mingled. By concentrating upon character, too, he introduced strong elements of drama. Once again Chaucer seems to be the progenitor of a national style.

Chapter Eight
Bloody Revolt

There is a curious double perspective in Chaucer's life which amounts almost to an optical illusion. We see him most clearly in minute particulars, in the context of very small events, but he withdraws himself from the larger picture. About the great events of the realm, he writes nothing. It is perhaps the natural result of his own self-effacement and canny neutrality.

Thus he appears in the public records, in February 1381, as the surety or 'mainprise' for a wealthy London merchant; John Hend was a draper who had seized some land in Essex, apparently unlawfully, but Chaucer was willing to guarantee his future good conduct. Among the other 'mainpernors', interestingly enough, was a man to whom Chaucer later dedicated *Troilus and Criseyde*. Ralph Strode was a philosopher and poet who, in this period, lived above Aldersgate in precisely the same circumstances as Chaucer above Aldgate. He was a lawyer and sergeant-at-law, like John Gower, and can be intimately identified with that urban circle of cultured lawyers and merchants of which Chaucer was a part. They were rich and successful citizens, and men of letters, whose professional careers were expressions of their general civility, and they must have comprised the most discriminating part of Chaucer's own audience.

So the name of Chaucer is associated with a small legal

affair in the early months of 1381. Nothing is known, however, about his conduct that year in the largest and most important civic insurrection in English history. On 13 June 1381, the disaffected peasants and disappointed rebels of the kingdom poured beneath Chaucer's lodgings in Aldgate and began the systematic sack of London; in later years it became known as 'the Peasants' Revolt', although many thousands of estranged Londoners joined the general riot. The proximate cause of their anger lay in the imposition of a 'poll tax', of three groats, on every individual, rich or poor. But there was also discontent at the attempt to fix the wage levels of a labouring population which had been much reduced by the 'death' of 1349; the working people were more mobile, and less loyal, than ever before. The revolt was in that sense a symptom of the final disruption of the feudal system of manorial authority. It represented a break with the past, and was perhaps inevitably accompanied by violence and murder.

Geoffrey Chaucer, as collector of customs, was exactly the kind of person the rebels were hunting down. They murdered the tax collectors and the most prominent servants of the young king. The palace of Chaucer's protector, John of Gaunt, was burned to the ground. Yet Chaucer escaped. If he did not go into hiding, he must have been in his lodgings above Aldgate. There is no evidence that he joined the fifteen-year-old king, Richard II, and his councillors who had retreated to safety in the Tower of London. He must, in the common phrase, have laid low and waited for the storm to pass. Lying low was, perhaps, one of his favourite positions. From that vantage he could have seen the rebel encampment at Mile End, from the window of his chamber, as well as the strongholds of the city erupting in flame.

The dramatic intervention of the king by riding to a meeting of the rebels in Smithfield, and the sudden killing in that place of the rebellion's leader, Wat Tyler, at the hands of the lord mayor, brought the rebellion to an unanticipated and in certain respects inconclusive end. The king, and his councillors, survived what had been the greatest threat to their authority since the reign of King John. Yet Chaucer, to all intents and purposes, never mentions the matter. There is only one stray allusion, in 'The Nun's Priest's Tale , to 'Jakke Straw and his meynee'

The peasants' revolt of 1381. The priest John Ball, on horseback, addresses the Kentish rebels. John Ball and Wat Tyler (left) are identified by their names on their coats

– Jack Straw was another of the rebels' leaders – who

> Ne made nevere shoutes half so shrille
> Whan that they wolden any Flemyng kille.

There is stray, and probably formulaic, description of the 'cherles rebellyng' in *The Canterbury Tales.* But that is all. It is as if it had never happened. Of course it may be an aesthetic matter. If there were no literary models or examples to hand, he may not have been able to employ this new material in a convincing way. His imagination demanded bright originals; otherwise, it became cold and

On the right, the fifteen-year-old king, Richard II, addresses the peasants. On the left, Lord Mayor Walworth cuts off Wat Tyler's head

inactive. It is not the first time it has been suggested that, in some sense, Chaucer had a passive or inert imagination that had to be quickened into life by some other literary vision. His general attitude to life may have been an unassuming or even blank one; it is very hard to see him holding any firm opinions, or engaging in moral judgement. His life would be shaped by the ordinances of others or the prescriptions of duty. His art would be formed in the reaction to, or absorption of, other pre-eminent influences.

From other allusions in his poetry, however, it is clear that Chaucer had no very high opinion of the London crowd. He considered it to be fickle and dangerous or, as he put it in 'The Clerk's Tale':

> O stormy peple! Unsad and evere untrewe!
> Ay undiscreet and chaungynge as a vane!
> Delitynge evere in rumbul that is newe,
> For lyk the moone ay wexe ye and wane!

All the evidence suggests that he was firmly in the camp of the civic and royal authorities. And why should he not be? He was becoming an affluent, as well as an eminent, citizen. On 19 June, just six days after the incursion of the rebels, he sold the deeds of the family house in Thames Street to its leaseholder. It is likely that the recent death of his mother allowed him to 'quitclaim' the property, but he was no doubt happy to do so in the shadow of contemporaneous events. The rebels had conceived a particular hatred for those foreign merchants in the city who were favoured by the crown and by the tax collectors. On the day after their incursion into London they besieged thirty-five Flemings who were taking refuge in the church of St Martin in the Vintry, and removed them by force; it will be remembered that this was the church beside Chaucer's family home, in which the poet himself had possibly been baptised. The merchants and their families were then beheaded in the street, and their bodies left to rot. It was said that Wat Tyler himself was searching for one particular Flemish merchant, Sir Richard Lyons, who was the close friend and quondam employer of Chaucer himself. It is a particularly strident example of the violence of medieval life, a violence which in every sense reached Chaucer's own doorstep. Yet in his own reference to the murdered Flemings, already quoted, he seems extraordinarily detached from the events in question.

The profit he made on the sale of the family house was added to further gains. Only three weeks before he had been granted a gift of some sixteen pounds by his grateful employers; he was assigned moneys due to the exchequer from various crown debtors, a measure which can only have been authorised by the king or the king's councillors. He had also just received some twenty-two pounds in payment for his earlier journeys to France, and in the previous year he had been awarded the balance of his costs for the journey to Milan.

It is perhaps peculiar, then, that he should receive an 'advance' on his annuity of 6s 8d just two months after selling the family house, together with another advance in November of the same year. It is not at all clear why he needed these small extra sums. Lovers of domestic drama might suggest that it had something to do with the claims of Cecily Champain upon him.

Chapter Nine
The Affairs of Troy

If Richard II proved his courage by confronting the dissidents in the summer of 1381, his marriage to Anne of Bohemia in 1382 set the seal of stability upon what was now a recognised and recognisable royal court. It initiated what was in many respects a magnificent period, even though it ended in the forced abdication and murder of Richard himself. If a reign is also to be celebrated for the culture which it creates, then that of Richard must be remembered for the work of Langland and of Gower no less than that of Chaucer himself. It was a resplendent literary period, only to be equalled by that of Elizabeth in the late sixteenth century. It was the age of a masterpiece such as 'the Wilton Diptych'. It was the first age of the mystery plays. It was the age of the great religious works of Margery Kempe and Julian of Norwich. It was the context for the 'East Anglian revival' both in manuscript illumination and in wall-painting. Richard II had a fully conceived and almost theatrical sense of his own kingship; he believed that he ruled by divine authority and was inspired by the divine will. It was a court of ceremony and of formal ritual; it was no longer a court of war in anything but a theoretical sense. This in turn encouraged what might be called the self-consciousness of the nation, so that all aspects of the body politic came to be represented in dramatic or rhetorical terms. No other medieval king can boast of such a legacy. To this must be added the influence at the English court of Milan and Bohemia, of Genoa and Paris, of Provence and Pavia. Chaucer was part of this European tradition but it ought to be remembered that he owed as much to the demotic of the mystery plays as to the rhetoric of Dante or of Petrarch. He was at the heart of both a national and an international culture.

This is nowhere more evident than in the poem which he began to compose during this period. *Troilus and Criseyde* has been hailed as the first novel in modern English. But it is more than that. It is a love story and a farce, a lament and a philosophical enquiry, a social comedy and a threnody upon destiny; it is a novel of manners and a poem of high deeds. It is a commodious and accommodating epic poem, and such a new thing in English that it can really be given no fixed or definite name. It can only be said, perhaps, that it is the first modern work of literature in English. In a sense it can be described as an epic of Englishness itself, since it is such an absorbent and accommodating, assimilative and heterogeneous, work of art.

By common consent its origin is to be found in Boccaccio's *Il Filostrato*. It is the ground of Chaucer's endeavour, and there are numerous indications that he was engaged in a very close reading of the Italian poem. Indeed all the evidence suggests that he had the volume open before him, since there are many line-by-line translations which could not have been accomplished by memory alone. In particular the openings of Chaucer's stanzas are closely modelled upon Boccaccio's own words, as if Chaucer needed the lift and inspiration of the original before

The Wilton Diptych of 1395–99: one of the great works of art to be produced in the reign of Richard II, who is shown with his

patron saint, John the Baptist, and saints Edward and Edmund
being presented to the Virgin and Child

embarking upon his own invention and transvaluation. The lines:

> Tu stai negli occhi suoi, signor verace
> sì come in loco degno a tua virtute

become in Chaucer's poem:

> Ye stonden in hir eighen myghtily,
> As in a place unto youre vertu digne . . .

This is very close translation indeed, where relatively unfamiliar words such as 'vertu' and 'digne' had to be employed in order to follow the Italian closely. Indeed the whole of *Il Filostrato* shines through *Troilus and Criseyde* as the permanent fabric of Chaucer's venture.

The story itself is an old one, lingering in the European imagination since the middle of the twelfth century as a token of disappointed love and doomed civilisation. The unhappy story is set in Troy just before its destruction at the hands of the Greek invaders. Her father having gone over to the side of the besiegers, Criseyde is left alone and bereft in her native city; Troilus, one of the heroes of the Trojan army, falls wholly and irrevocably in love with this solitary figure. They become lovers – in Chaucer's version by the machinations of Criseyde's uncle, Pandarus – and enjoy a brief period of ecstatic happiness. Then it is decreed by the civic authorities that Criseyde should be despatched to her father and to the Greek camp in exchange for certain Trojan worthies; the parting of Troilus and Criseyde in which Criseyde pledges by her truth and her honour to remain ever faithful to Troilus is one of the great moments of European literature, rivalling the scenes between Tristram and Isolde. When she is comfortably ensconced in the Greek camp, however, she reneges upon her solemn promise in order to pursue her passion for the warrior Diomede. After weary watchings and searchings for her, Troilus eventually realises the extent of her iniquity and dies of a broken heart. In Chaucer's version, however, he is lifted into the eighth sphere and realises at last the futility of all earthly love and the vicissitudes of all worldly fortune. It is a wonderful story, which had been transmitted through every generation of poets and minstrels. It was only when Chaucer read *Il Filostrato*, however, that he was deeply impressed with the possibilities of the theme. It might almost be said that he was engaged in a competitive act with the older Italian poet, by trying to prove that he could outwrite him upon his own ground. The differences between the two poems might then be seen as the difference between the work of a young Italian, and the work of a middle-aged English, poet. But there are more subtle contrasts.

Chaucer's alterations and additions to *Il Filostrato*, for example, are of some significance in any account of his poetic genius. Boccaccio wrote the poem when he was still in his twenties, and it is designed in part to be an account of the narrator's own love-sickness at the departure of his mistress from Naples. Chaucer removes any personal application and instead introduces a narrator who is somewhat bewildered by the course of events and who in no sense feels that he is a part of them; he is a somewhat bookish creature, referring back to his authorities and disavowing any private opinion on the matters discussed:

Men seyn – I not – that she yaf hym hire herte.

It is only to be expected that Chaucer deepens and strengthens the characterisation of the major actors, principally by means of irony and comedy; the constant emphasis lies between the words and the deeds, between the professions of love or honesty and the actual dissimulation involved in any act of love. Chaucer turns a romance into a drama, with all the subtleties of character and action that this requires.

He also emphasises the feudal and medieval aspects of the tale. In Boccaccio's account it almost becomes a modern love story, but in Chaucer's rendering it reassumes all the trappings of antiquity and ritual courtesy. This is part of the general English instinct for antiquarianism in all of its forms, but it had the added virtue of imbuing the poem with that bookishness or literariness which was very much to Chaucer's taste. In the same spirit the English poet also introduced the concept of Fate or Destiny as one of the primary agents of the narrative; there are occasions when the two lovers, and indeed the two warring hosts, seem to be the helpless subjects of forces which they can neither control nor understand. Chaucer also introduces astrological and astronomical lore as a way of preserving the mysteries of fortune in a story of love which can have no happy ending. These higher powers can of course induce a sense of tragedy or a sense of irony; it says much about Chaucer's genius that in this poem he is capable of both.

He had in fact been translating a philosophical treatise on the nature of fortune even as he was composing the poem itself. *The Consolation of Philosophy* by Boethius, the sixth-century Roman philosopher, was one of the key medieval texts. Indeed its appeal to an English audience predated the fourteenth century. King Alfred had also translated the work some five hundred years before. But for Chaucer it seems to have had some private, as well as public, significance. Its principal theme lies in the need to reach the home and haven of 'Philiosophie' as a way of forgetting the uncertain delights of 'the blynde goddesse Fortune'; the text was written while Boethius, the servant of a sixth-century king, lay awaiting death in a prison cell. It has all the force and bitterness of private sorrow within it. Only by embracing the serene precepts of philosophy is it possible to escape 'the swyftnesse and the sweighe' of worldly fortune's 'turnynge wheel'.

The injunction of philosophy – 'Hope aftir no thyng, ne drede nat' – also seems perfectly appropriate to one of Chaucer's quiet or at least quietistic temperament. He may be imagined to be something of a fatalist in the affairs of the world, who welcomed a treatise that encouraged a settled *contemptus mundi* in the face of trials or privations. He may not have progressed as far in his public career as he had hoped or expected; he may have willingly disavowed that career in order to serve his poetic vocation. Whatever the truth of the matter he would have been only too happy to dismiss 'thilke merveylous monstre Fortune'. By gaining tranquillity of soul 'thow art myghty over thyself'. The treatise then proceeds to a debate on the relative status of human free will and divine providence; it is central to fourteenth-century theological speculation, but at this late date it is enough to say that it was resolved to the satisfaction of Chaucer himself. Providence is the scheme of all created things as it exists in the mind of God, for whom the thing that men call 'time' does not exist. Free will can be exercised as this eternal scheme works itself through the changeable things in time. It is the philosophical equivalent of a double-edged sword.

The language of Boethius's work enters many of Chaucer's shorter poems in this period, and has a direct bearing upon the epic fable of 'Palamon and Arcite' which he was also composing; that poem eventually emerges as 'The Knight's Tale' in *The Canterbury Tales*, so the influence of Boethius can be said to have lingered until his last years. But the period of the early 1380s can still justly be called the period of his philosophical poetry. The vocabulary of Boethius is introduced within *Troilus and Criseyde* in a direct manner, for example, in Troilus's oration upon 'necessite' and 'Goddes prescience eternel'; that great verse disquisition is followed by the entry of Pandarus with his own brand of worldly wisdom. In this context it is important to realise that the poetic language and tone of *Troilus and Criseyde* are entirely flexible; they contain Saxon and Romance elements in such a degree of mutual compatibility that they can be shaped in any way.

The distinction between rhetoric and ordinary speech in fact conveys half of the poem's meaning, since the narrative is conducted by means of orations which speak less than the truth. It is impossible not to be reminded of Chaucer's own career in royal service, where he would have been expected to use his skills as a rhetorician in order to fabricate a courtly or civilised reality beyond the imperatives of power and commerce. The poem itself is filled with false words or brittle words that do not bear much investigation. Words become dangerous when they are bewitching. 'I shal hym so enchaunten with my sawes,' Criseyde declares, and, in turn, it is said that 'ravysshen he shal yow with his speche'. *Troilus and Criseyde* is a drama of duplicity. It presents a world established upon etiquette and the rituals of social appearance, while the most significant events take place *sub rosa* or, in the medieval phrase, under the thumb:

> Ye knowe al thilke covered qualitee
> Of thynges, which that folk on wondren so.

When his characters are confronted with the truth of their actions or words they are embarrassed; they go red, or they sit 'as stil as any ston'.

This emphasis upon oration, and the 'covered qualitee' of speech, lends weight to the argument that *Troilus and Criseyde* was indeed designed for oral delivery. There are references in the text which seem to support such a conclusion, particularly when Chaucer can be presumed to be addressing an audience:

> For ay the ner the fir, the hotter is –
> This, trowe I, knoweth al this compaignye.

What 'compaignye' can it be, other than that sitting before him? And again he talks directly to his hearers:

> For sothe, I have naught herd it don er this
> In story non, ne no man here, I wene . . .

The possibilities of performance are of course infinite in such a context. It has often been suggested that there are so many areas of irony and ambiguity in Chaucer's poem that it is impossible to gauge or gather any one 'meaning' from the work; that is why it has been interpreted in a hundred different ways. But if you consider the poem as a text for performance, in which the narrator conveys meaning by gesture or expression, many of the apparent difficulties of interpretation can be resolved. The voices of Criseyde and Pandarus are literally equivocal – their real feelings and motives are not disclosed – but a competent actor would bring them fully to life. We may assume, indeed, that Chaucer himself was just such a performer. He was an actor in his daily life, adopting the roles of diplomat and negotiator, and he may have extended his skills into more formal productions.

He may have acted the parts of *Troilus and Criseyde* in front of a courtly gathering, but he may also have narrated the poem before an urban audience. There was an annual feast for the city merchants, known from French derivation as a 'puy', when 'royal songs' were performed in a form of oratorical contest; it was very much a medieval affair, again not unlike the debates in the Inns of Court, and can be understood as one of the sources of Tudor drama. It is also a lively social context in which we may see Geoffrey Chaucer. It is perhaps the best explanation for the poem's dedication to John Gower and Ralph Strode, both of them sergeants-at-law and both of them members of what might be called the civic aristocracy.

But nothing can ever be exactly known. There are allusions in *Troilus and Criseyde*, for example, which suggest that the poem was also conceived as a text or book to be perused by the solitary reader:

> Thow, redere, maist thiself ful wel devyne
> That swich a wo my wit kan nat diffyne . . .

There is a short poem of the period, addressed to a scrivener named Adam:

> Adam scriveyn, if ever it thee bifalle
> Boece or Troylus for to wryten newe,
> Under thy long lokkes thou most have the scalle,
> But after my makyng thow wryte more trewe.

The poet is here complaining about the faulty state of Adam's copies, which he must 'rubbe and scrape' to correct and to refine. It is further evidence that *Troilus and Criseyde* was indeed circulated in manuscript form. It was a text for contemplation as well as performance; Chaucer was, as in so many other respects, on the cusp of two worlds. He was poised between the courtly poet, who declaimed his verses in the hall after vespers, and the self-conscious literary artist.

It is natural and inevitable that we should return here to the illustration that is the frontispiece to one edition of *Troilus and Criseyde*. The entire scene, of the poet in a pulpit addressing his noble audience, is to be interpreted in the context of reading as preaching; we are aware that Chaucer is in earnest as well as game, to use one of his own favourite contrasts, and that he is engaged in the formation of 'high sentence' as part of his ethical intention. He is as interested in 'sentence' as in 'solas'. It has been suggested that two figures in front of the decorated pulpit are engaged in miming the action which Chaucer is expounding; this possibility would throw an interesting light upon the circumstances of poetic delivery. But the audience are indeed primarily auditors. They are engaged in a communal act, with its own rules and expectations. The poet will address those gathered before him in ways which engage and hold their attention. The verses, as Chaucer put it, are 'red wherso thow be, or elles songe'. Sometimes he will address them directly in inspired or impassioned terms, so that he takes on all the skills of an orator. On other occasions he will become more familiar, with sly anecdote or innuendo; he will then be less of an impersonal orator than the individual Geoffrey Chaucer, the frail mortal whose idiosyncrasies will be known to some of the audience. There are any number of strategies or subtleties which can also be introduced; Chaucer may impersonate another speaker, or by his expression and gesture contradict the apparent import of his words. That is why it has proved impossible to interpret Chaucer's written texts in any fixed or coherent manner; every critic has his or her own theory. Without the performer, where is the meaning? And what is the use of critical explication, when the poems reveal themselves always in fresh and unanticipated ways?

At the end of *Troilus and Criseyde* there is an apostrophe to his own poetry:

> Go, litel bok, go, litel myn tragedye,
> Ther God thi makere yet, er that he dye,
> So sende myght to make in som comedye!
> But litel book, no makyng thow n'envie,

> But subgit be to alle poesye;
> And kis the steppes where as thow seest pace
> Virgile, Ovide, Omer, Lucan, and Stace.

This may be an anticipation of the 'comedye' of his last years, *The Canterbury Tales*, but perhaps more importantly Chaucer is here aspiring towards a place in the pantheon of the great poets. He had alluded to them before. In *The House of Fame* Statius and Lucan, Virgil and Homer, were all holding up the glory and burden of their respective civilisations. They represented 'alle poesye' but they also embodied the gifts and aspirations of their nations. There can be little doubt that Chaucer now considered himself to be worthy of the same company. He was quite aware of his achievement in *Troilus and Criseyde*, and was, as it were, asserting his claim to being the poetic representative or poetic authority of England.

Chapter Ten
Residence in Kent

Chaucer had by now acquired a considerable reputation. In this period his younger contemporary, Thomas Usk, wrote of 'the noble philosophicall poete in Englissh' and his 'boke of Troilus'; at the same time the French poet, Eustache Deschamps, saluted him as '*Ovides grans en ta poeterie*', the Ovid of your poetry. In the poem that succeeded *Troilus and Criseyde*, *The Legend of Good Women*, Alcestis commands the poet thus:

> And whan this book ys maad, yive it the quene,
> On my byhalf, at Eltham or at Sheene.

We may surmise, therefore, that Chaucer's poetry would not be unwelcome at the royal palaces. As a reward or recognition of his services, perhaps, he had been appointed controller of the petty custom in the spring of 1382. He had been granted that post eight years before, but not as part of any permanent arrangement. Now it had become a more secure source of income. The fact that in the following month he was allowed to name a deputy suggests that it had also become something of a sinecure; the deputy would do the work, for an appropriate sum, and Chaucer would collect the fee. It was an old medieval custom, reflected also in the number of benefices available in the Church. In the following year Chaucer was also granted a deputy for the controllership of the wool custom and subsidy, on the grounds that he was '*grandement occupez*' with '*certeines ses busoignes*'– greatly occupied with other necessary matters. It has been surmised that this other business was the completion of *Troilus and Criseyde*, but he may simply have been growing tired of the occupation of customs official. It is also possible that he was once more engaged upon the king's 'secret business'. Another deputy, for more general matters pertaining to the customs house, was appointed in 1384 to cover Chaucer's absence for a month on affairs unspecified. On 17 February 1385, a permanent deputy was installed. The records represent a gradual if steady withdrawal from the busy and sometimes perilous world of the Port of London. It would have been a noisy, as well as a busy, world. During this period the customs house was being extensively rebuilt; a new counting-house, and a new latrine, were some of the additions. Yet during these years of semi-detached attendance, Chaucer was not entirely free of duties. He still had to view the accounts, and ultimately to take responsibility for them to the exchequer. The audits and bills are presented '*per visum et testimonium Galfridi Chaucer*'. On one occasion, when his name was left off from an account, he had to appear in person – '*in propria persona sua*' – to take an oath regarding its authenticity.

His wife was certainly not 'in propria persona'. Far from being at her husband's side, Philippa Chaucer had joined her sister, Katherine Swynford, in her house in Lincolnshire; as John of Gaunt's mistress Katherine was in charge of a large household, and all the evidence suggests that Philippa was resident there for some years. Her annuities were paid in Lincolnshire in 1378; she was admitted to the fraternity of Lincoln Cathedral in 1386. For a period of at least eight years, therefore, she is connected with that county. These were also the years in which Chaucer was residing above Aldgate, and cover the period when he was in some form of legal contention with Cecily Champain. It is hard to escape the conclusion that he led a somewhat unconventional marital life.

Husband and wife would have been reunited, however, for the funeral of Princess Joan, the mother of Richard II, in January 1386. There is an account of the great wardrobe giving details of the black cloth granted to Chaucer for the livery of mourning; interestingly enough, the poet is classed with esquires and sergeants-at-law, which testifies once more to Chaucer's high status in fourteenth-century England; to be an esquire was to be one rank below that of knight. Since Princess Joan had exercised her influence on John of Gaunt's behalf on several occasions and had in addition been close to Philippa's old mistress, Queen Philippa, Chaucer's wife would undoubtedly have been at the same courtly ceremony. Whether the pair exchanged ritual kisses, or whether they recognised some more intimate bond, is not known. In the late medieval period there is the strangest amalgam of theoretical devotion and cool practicality – between the ready emotionalism of Chaucer's love poetry, for example, and the more pragmatic arrangements between husband and wife.

The queen had in fact died in the autumn of 1385, her funeral delayed by matters of state, during which period Chaucer was appointed a Justice with the Commission of the

Peace for Kent. His predecessor, Thomas de Shardelowe, had been the king's coroner and attorney in the King's Bench; Chaucer had become part of a distinguished tradition. It is another measure of his standing in the relatively small community of medieval administrators, and an indication that he was not known solely or simply for his poetry. He was, before all else, a man of affairs; he was, in the words of the Statute of Cambridge, one of 'the best and most lawful men'. As a Justice of the Peace he would sit in judgement upon the transgression of civic laws, such as 'regrating' or profiteering and offences against the statute of labourers, or in the preliminary investigation of more serious offences, such as rape or murder, which would subsequently be tried in the London courts. His colleagues were men of substance and reputation, among them peers and king's councillors, but he would in certain instances have acted as an independent justice. His appointment does not necessarily imply, but it does suggest, that he was well versed in matters of law; it gives some strength to the argument that at some earlier point in his life he was instructed at an Inn of Court. It is perhaps also worth noting, in the light of Chaucer's subsequent verse, that he is likely to have travelled to Canterbury on many occasions; the route which his pilgrims took was one that had become very familiar to him.

Chaucer's association with Kent became more obvious at a later date, when he left Aldgate for Greenwich, but he could scarcely have been named as Justice of the Peace for that county if he was not in residence there. It has been argued that the king had appointed Chaucer to be steward of the royal palaces at Eltham and at Sheen; they are both situated in Kent and, if the surmise were to prove correct, they provided an appropriate link with the county. It is a theory which at least has the merit of consistency. Other Justices of the Peace had been stewards of great men, and earned a place upon the bench as their representatives. It would also form an appropriate prelude to Chaucer's later appointment by the king as clerk of the king's works. We may possibly imagine the poet, then, living for some of the time in a manor upon one of the royal estates.

Further public recognition was bestowed upon him in the year succeeding his appointment as Justice of the Peace. In the summer of 1386 he was nominated as a Member of Parliament for Kent as an honorary 'knight of the shire'. His brief membership of that Parliament is well enough attested. It met, in the Great Chapter House of Westminster Abbey, on the first day of October, and became known as the 'Wonderful Parliament'; it gained this honorific by demanding tighter scrutiny of the king's expenditure and by curtailing the privileges and powers of the king's chief ministers. Chaucer had of course been despatched there as a king's man – all his affluence and prestige flowed directly from the court – and would have attended the proceedings as a hapless and unhappy witness. His discomfiture was no doubt increased by a petition presented to this Parliament which demanded that the controllers of customs at the English ports – or at least those appointed for life – should be disciplined or dismissed because of their manifest corruption. The leader of the revolt against the king, his uncle the duke of Gloucester, was in fact owed five hundred pounds by the customs which Chaucer himself controlled. Although he had not been appointed for life at the Port of

London, he might justifiably have considered himself a direct target of Parliament's complaints.

Four days after the Parliament met he gave up the lease to his lodgings in Aldgate. It was a coincidence of timing, but it was not a coincidence of planning. He was already engaged in steady withdrawal from the work of the Port of London, as has been noticed, and his removal from Aldgate was the preliminary step to giving up the controllership altogether. He may have anticipated the general assault upon the king's controllers, and removed himself from the scene of the contention, but this is unlikely. No one could have anticipated the actions of the 'Wonderful Parliament' in that much detail. It is possible that he was actively encouraged to leave his post by Gloucester and by others, but he was in any case growing more detached from the office. His only interest lay in its income.

He had already vacated Aldgate by the time he surrendered the lease to his successor, Richard Forster, on 5 October; since he was soon known to be a resident of Kent it seems likely that he had moved to that county. He is named in a Kentish legal action as early as 13 November, 1386, in connection with some men of Greenwich; there is some evidence that one of these men, Simon Manning, was married to a sister of Chaucer. An official document of 1419, concerning a Kent Visitation, contains the sentence, '*Simon Manning de Codham, superstes 46 E.3 et 5 R.2 = Catherina soror Galfridi Chawcer militis celeberimi poetae Anglicani*'. Katherine Chaucer herself remains obscure. It is not even known if she could read. As a Justice of the Peace in 1387 her brother sat at Dartford, in Kent, and in the following year an exchequer action against him was heard in the same county. In another legal document of the same year he is noted as being 'of the county of Kent'. The evidence, then, is conclusive. It seems likely that he migrated to Greenwich, or to the neighbouring town of Deptford, in which vicinity he remained for the next thirteen years. These were the years of *The Canterbury Tales*, in which Chaucer alludes to his own neighbourhood:

> Lo Depeford, and it is half-wey pryme!
> Lo Grenewych, ther many a shrewe is inne!
> It were al tyme thy tale to bigynne.

No doubt he had particular 'shrewes' in mind.

There was no forced retreat from London, however, in the autumn of 1386. He had left Aldgate on 5 October, but he must have found sufficiently comfortable lodgings elsewhere in the city. On 15 October, in the middle of the 'Wonderful Parliament' he was called to give evidence in a case of some celebrity. He was a witness in an action brought against Sir Robert Grosvenor by Sir Richard Scrope over the right to bear a certain coat of arms. The trial took place in the refectory of Westminster Abbey, so Chaucer would have walked from the chapter-house where the Parliament was assembled in order to make his deposition. Chaucer gave evidence on behalf of Scrope, whom he had known over the years as an armed knight and as a courtier. They had both served in France twenty-seven years before, and Chaucer testified that the plaintiff had then carried the arms currently in dispute. But a more immediate, and more interesting, part of his testimony concerned his perambulations around London.

It is likely that he gave his evidence in 'law French', a corrupted form of Anglo-Norman, and we may even hear him talking in this transcription: '*il dist qil estoit une foitz en Fridaystrete en Liundres com il alast en la rewe . . .*', he said that he was once in Friday Street and as he was walking along the street . . . Chaucer saw the said coat of arms hanging outside a house. He asked if these were the arms of the Scropes when '*un autre luy respondist et dit: Nenyl sieur*', another person answered him and said Not at all, sir. He was told: These are the arms of Sir Robert Grosvenor. Chaucer then averred that '*ceo fuist le primer foitz*', it was the first time, that he had ever heard of Grosvenor. At this late date the niceties of the matter are of no importance; Scrope eventually won the case, no doubt by the claim of reputation rather than of justice. But the shape of Chaucer's testimony is interesting. He gives his evidence in the form of a little story – the stranger in Friday Street, the forthright response, the personal demurral. It is all of a piece with what we know, or suspect, of his character in the world. He may even have imitated the voice of the Londoner who expostulated, '*Nenyl sieur*'.

He formally resigned his offices as controller in the last days of 1386. On 4 December he gave up the controllership of the wool custom, and ten days later he relinquished his post as controller of the petty custom; his successors, Adam Yardley and Henry Gisors, were known to him as city men of repute. He had served in the Port of London for more than twelve years; only one controller had served longer. The duration of his office suggests Chaucer's adaptability as well as his efficiency, in other words, and further royal appointments would soon be bestowed upon him.

In this period of change and instability, however, he attended continually to his poetry. There are short poems attributed to him, among them a work entitled 'Lak of Stedfastnesse' which has been considered as an address to Richard II. One copy of the poem has an 'envoy' or postscript to the young king:

> O prince, desyre to be honourable,
> Cherish thy folk and hate extorcioun.

Another short poem, 'Truth', has the distinction of being Chaucer's most popular lyric in subsequent years. It is suffused with Boethian doctrine and is composed of memorable lines:

> Her is non hoom, her nis but wildernesse:
> Forth, pilgrim, forth! Forth, beste, out of thy stal!

At some point in this period, too, he began work on a translation of Pope Innocent III's treatise *De miseria condicionis humane*, otherwise known as *De contemptu mundi*. The title was translated by Chaucer himself as *Of the Wreched Engendrynge of Mankynde*, which may give some clue to its morbid and penitential contents. The translation itself has not survived, but the fact that the poet must have pored over it word by word – transmitting it, as it were, into the centre of his own creativity – is suggestive enough. On one level such a pious and lachrymose work must have deeply appealed to his own sensibility. It is an apt rejoinder to those who believe that 'The Parson's Tale' is too gloomy an ending to *The Canterbury Tales*. On the contrary,

Chaucer may have seen it as the perfect summation for the caricature of a wicked world. There is always a certain darkness within Chaucer's merriment; like many other artists his comic genius may have been in part inspired by an unhappy and obsessive temperament.

Chaucer's principal efforts in this period, however, were devoted to another long poem. The success of *Troilus and Criseyde* must have emboldened him to embark upon another comprehensive poetic work, although one conceived in quite a different manner. It was entitled *The Legend of Good Women.*

Queen Dido. Nineteenth-century tapestry panel designed by William Morris to illustrate Chaucer's *The Legend of Good Women*

It is a court poem; it was dedicated to Queen Anne, and may well have been commissioned by her. The theme lies in its celebration of women who have died or been betrayed for love: the fates of Dido, Philomela, and Cleopatra are among those lamented in a series of short verse biographies. Chaucer meets in dream the god and queen of love; the god berates him for writing of love's failures, and the queen requests him to compose threnodies of those good women who had been abandoned or destroyed. Chaucer is once more concerned with the revision of old stories, or familiar legends, for a contemporary audience. That is perhaps enough in itself to identify *The Legend* with the court, where such material was considered to be the *materia prima* of poetry itself. It seems in every sense to have been a command performance. John Gower was charged with precisely the same task in his *Confessio Amantis*, where a series of love-tales are finished within an elaborate frame in which the poet meets the king and queen of love. Gower even describes the occasion when Richard II met him, when they were both sailing upon the Thames. 'He bad me come in to his barge' and thereupon 'this charge upon me leid'. It is more than coincidence that the two greatest poets of the age should embark upon the same task at the same time. It suggests a definite commission. In *Confessio Amantis*, too, John Gower delivers to Chaucer a message from the queen of love:

> And gret wel Chaucer whan ye mete,
> As mi disciple and mi poete.

There seems to be here some elaborate game of cross-reference, between two poems upon the same theme. It is a testimony to Chaucer's influence, too, that Gower chose to compose *Confessio Amantis* in English; it was the first time he had written a long poem in the vernacular (and indeed in the octosyllabic couplets which Chaucer employed in *The House of Fame*), and he must have been emboldened by Chaucer's considerable example and not inconsiderable success.

The legends themselves have been abbreviated so that they might easily fall within the scope of an evening's reading, and there are several references to elaborate court games and rituals. There is a wonderful encomium upon the daisy, for example, which refers to the cult of the *marguerite* imported from France. It has also been surmised that the 'ladyes nyntene' who accompany the god of love are in fact the nineteen ladies who had been enrolled in the Order of the Garter at the time of the poem's composition. There is also the type of humour which is best suited to personal delivery:

> Syn yit this day men may ensaumple se;
> And trusteth, as in love, no man but me.

There is also a suggestion of oral delivery in one of Chaucer's asides:

> But in this hous if any fals lovere be,
> Ryght as hymself now doth, ryght so dide he.

We may, then, still safely imagine Chaucer to be the favourite poet of the royal family.

The precise date of composition is not known, but internal evidence suggests that *The Legend of Good Women* was written at some time between *Troilus and Criseyde* and *The Canterbury Tales*. *The Legend* itself purports to be an act of atonement for Chaucer's description of the infidelity of Criseyde in the earlier poem. *The Canterbury Tales* is anticipated in the form of the decasyllabic couplet, which Chaucer employs with confidence and delicacy; as generations of English poets have since discovered, it is the perfect medium for conveying the rushing power of speech as well as the more ornate cadences of interior monologue. The compilation of so many different legends under the rubric of one general theme also testifies to Chaucer's innate love of difference and diversity. It is the key to his creativity. Just as *The Canterbury Tales* harbours many different kinds of story and story-teller, so *The Legend of Good Women* includes an extraordinary range of material from the myth of Philomela to the more carnal story of Cleopatra. They are all considered to be tales within a 'frame', old stories within a new framework; in that respect they resemble other great cultural artefacts of the period, such as the familiar words and letters of the gospels within the newly illuminated borders of a medieval manuscript. Chaucer seemed also to relish the prospect of intricacies within an overall pattern, like the Anglo-Saxon 'interlace' of his forebears. If there are general differences, there are also diverse particulars. The music of high lament is interrupted by asides of a more direct nature:

'Have at thee, Jason! Now thyn horn is blowe!'

And the cunningly wrought narrative is sometimes abruptly discarded for what seem to be expressions of private frustration with the sources:

> But whoso axeth who is with hym gon,
> Lat hym go rede Argonautycon,
> For he wole telle a tale long ynogh.

Chaucer, like two of his great successors Charles Dickens and William Shakespeare, can move from high tragedy to low comedy in the space of a phrase or a stanza without losing any control over his narrative. His is the genius of heterogeneity or what Dickens called the technique of 'streaky bacon'.

This is nowhere more evident than in the prologue to *The Legend of Good Women*. It survives in two versions, commonly known as 'F' and 'G'. The 'G' version appears to have been written after the death of Queen Anne in the summer of 1394; all references to her are excised, no doubt in deference to the king's grief, and 'my lady' becomes 'Alceste'. Her death so profoundly affected the king that he ordered the destruction of the manor at Sheen, which was so closely associated with his wife's happiness that he could no longer endure the sight of it. Chaucer may have also mourned. It has been suggested that, upon news of her death, he finally abandoned work upon *The Legend*. He was undoubtedly present at her funeral.

The lily is introduced in the later version, however, in celebration of the *fleur de lis* and the king's subsequent marriage to Princess Isabella of France. This late date also suggests that Chaucer was still returning to the poem long after he had started *The Canterbury Tales*; the fact that *The Legend* remains unfinished also suggests that it remained by his side for many years. In the poem itself he pledges to complete one legend each year, so that in a sense it must remain perpetually incomplete until the time of his death. The prologue is also significant for the fact that Chaucer enters the poem in a direct fashion. He is one of the protagonists who must plead his case before the god of love. Once more he portrays himself as a somewhat dull-witted and faint-hearted creature who bears no responsibility for what he utters. As Alceste, the queen of love, pleads in his defence:

> But for he useth bokes for to make,
> And taketh non hed of what matere he take,
> Therfore he wrot the Rose and ek Crisseyde
> Of innocence, and nyste what he seyde.
> Or hym was boden make thilke tweye
> Of som persone, and durst it not withseye.

In the last two lines he is suggesting that his translation of the *Roman de la rose*, and his composition of *Troilus and Crisyede*, were the result of his being 'boden' or commanded to write them. There is no external evidence to support this contention, which may be some kind of private joke, but it does help to illuminate the context in which Chaucer worked. He did not necessarily approach a theme or a story out of private considerations; he may have been commissioned, like any royal servant, to work upon worthwhile enterprises. It is also worthy of note that by writing a prologue devoted to his incapacity he manages to advert to his own poems, and to the whole arc of his professional career, without the taint of self-advertisement. It is yet another of his diplomatic accomplishments.

*

In the summer of 1387 those skills were required in a more obvious way; he was despatched to Calais in the king's service, and travelled with the Captain of Calais, but the nature of his business is unknown. He could not have remained there for very long, since in the following month he was in Dartford where he was acting as a justice *ad inquirendum*; Isabella Hall had been abducted by her husband, John Lording, from the custody of Thomas Carshill at Chislehurst. Lording was, however, rescuing his wife from a previous abduction conducted by Carshill himself. It must have been a sufficiently interesting case at the time, and the repeated use of the phrase '*rapuerunt et abduxerunt*' may have stirred Chaucer's memories of a court hearing in which he himself had once been involved.

In this period Philippa Chaucer died. It is perhaps appropriate for a woman about whom so little is known that her death can only be adduced from the absence of official records; her life annuity is no longer paid after 18 June 1387. She probably died at her sister's house in Lincolnshire, but no other circumstances can be recovered. Chaucer never mentioned her death in any public way, except insofar as he wrote one or two short poems in which he declared his intention never to remarry – never 'to falle of weddynge in the trappe'. It would seem that he had no very high opinion of the matrimonial state. Yet Philippa's influence may have had a more enduring legacy. Some of the narratives in *The Canterbury Tales* have been classified as 'the Marriage Group'; the tales of the Franklin and the Merchant, among others, are concerned with the theme of 'maistrie' or the battle for supremacy between husband and wife. It was one of Chaucer's abiding concerns and, despite their long if not permanent separation, may in part have been derived from Philippa's presence in his life.

Chaucer himself can often only be glimpsed in official records. On two occasions in 1388, for example, he was sued for debt. This was not an unusual circumstance for a middle-aged man in the late fourteenth century, but it does at least emphasise that the poet was by no means as affluent as the courtiers and London merchants with whom he had dealings. In the spring an exchequer action was taken against him by a grocer, John Churchman, for a debt of £3 6s 8d; in the following autumn a plea of debt was registered against Chaucer, for the sum of £7 13s 4d, by Henry Atwood. Atwood's occupation was given as 'hostelere' or inn-keeper, and it seems likely that Chaucer had taken a chamber in his inn when he had business in London. The eventual outcome of the suit is unknown, but it seems that Chaucer reached some private arrangement with Atwood. On this, the records are silent. It says something about the complicated forensic environment of the time that, in the same legal term as Chaucer was summoned to court for this debt, he himself was guaranteeing the appearance in court of Matilda Nemeg; she had been the victim of an abduction which, judging by the available records, was a most common offence in the period.

There was one other, and more important, legal process in this period. In the spring of 1388 Chaucer transferred all of his exchequer annuities to John Scalby; all of the payments made to him on the king's behalf were now to be given to Scalby, for which privilege Chaucer no doubt received a sum of money. The reasons for this transfer are obvious enough.

In the Parliament then sitting, known for its attacks upon the king's councillors as the 'Merciless Parliament', it was proposed that all annuities should be cancelled if the grantee had received any subsequent payments from the king. This was unfortunately Chaucer's case, and the threat that any future payments would be forfeit encouraged him to sell them as soon as possible. Once more he seems quick and efficient in the affairs of the world. That world, however, was now being turned upside-down.

Richard II was under severe threat from rebel lords and from the commons, to the extent that he may have been temporarily deposed. Certainly he was humiliated and threatened in the most obvious ways. Some of his closest and most important councillors were summarily tried and executed, among them friends of Chaucer himself. Sir Simon Burley and Nicholas Brembre, men whose names are closely connected to that of the poet in innumerable dealings, were beheaded. It must have occurred to Chaucer himself that he was safer in Greenwich than in London.

Chapter Eleven
The Tales of Canterbury

Chaucer now enjoyed a measure of space, and freedom, with which to contemplate the shape of his life and the direction of his poetry. He was poorer than he had been before, however, largely because he had relinquished his posts as controller and had given up his exchequer annuities. But he had more time and leisure at his disposal, and he was less concerned with the busy daily life of the city. He was not in retirement, but he was not continually occupied. It is no coincidence, therefore, that he first began to consider the possibilities of a frame narrative containing diverse tales. He was later to describe it as 'The Tales of Canterbury', and at an early stage he must have hit upon the device of a pilgrimage as a convenient context for the telling of stories and the interplay of various dramatic characters.

He had removed himself from the court, and *The Canterbury Tales* is the first long poem by Chaucer which does not have a courtly setting. The point could be put another way by suggesting that it was his first modern epic. Of course it is not 'realistic', in any contemporary sense, but it is the first long poem in English which takes as its subject the vagaries of daily life. Its only possible rival in this sphere, William Langland's *Piers the Plowman*, is a dream vision of religious import. *The Canterbury Tales* is a story of familiar characters in a recognisable setting.

By the time he had settled in Greenwich he had already written two of the tales, no doubt as independent poems; they became 'The Knight's Tale' concerning Palamon and Arcite and 'The Second Nun's Tale' on the life of St Cecile. But it is likely that at a very early stage he conceived of a great and open poem that would allow him to introduce a whole new range of material. In the early lines of the 'General Prologue' he addresses what by implication is a general readership:

> And made forward erly for to ryse,
> To take oure wey ther as I yow devyse.

The poem was never formally completed, and exists in a number of stray manuscripts and groups of manuscripts which have been knitted together by later commentators in various patterns. It is most likely that Chaucer never did finish work upon it, but considered it as somehow a permanent part of his creative career. Like life itself, it was accumulative and unpredictable.

The period during which he could bestow all his time and labour upon it, however, was relatively short. In the spring of 1389 Richard II shook off his opponents. He declared himself to be of age and pronounced himself fit and capable of exercising all the powers of the sovereign. It cannot be entirely coincidental that two months later, on 12 July 1389, Chaucer was appointed clerk of the king's works. This was a grand if arduous appointment (later held by such dignitaries as Sir Christopher Wren) which could have allowed Chaucer little leisure for his literary affairs. It was not a reward or sinecure for an old servant of the crown but, rather, a pressing and important duty imposed upon a skilful and sharp-witted administrator. It has been suggested that he had already become steward of the palaces of Eltham and of Sheen, which would at least be a fitting prelude to work in this new post. He had been appointed at the behest of the king himself, who in his resurgent position wished for a royal servant who could help him to maintain in a literal sense the fabric of his authority.

The clerk of the king's works was supposed to administer and oversee all building work upon the king's estates as well as to undertake necessary repairs to buildings, walls, fish-ponds and the other appurtenances of royal households. He also had to employ and pay the workmen, arrange for the purchase and safe delivery of the building supplies, and keep all the necessary accounts in good order. The details of the appointment include work 'at our Palace of Westminster, our Tower of London, our Castle of Berkhampstead, our Manors of Kennington, Eltham, Clarendon, Shene, Byfleet, Chiltern Langley, and Feckenham'. Chaucer had to appoint four deputies as well as purveyors and clerks; his own office was situated within the royal palace at Westminster. It must have been in every sense a full-time job, for which he was paid the not inconsiderable sum of two shillings a day. There are records of his dealings with the master mason, Henry Yevele; during this period Yevele was concerned with the design and construction of the nave in Westminster Abbey. There are other records concerning the master carpenter and the king's gardener, as well as various craftsmen and labourers, and in the accounts there are references to 'carriage of stone from Windsor Great Chapel' and 'repair of houses for weighing wool by the Tower'. Chaucer's principal responsibility in fact seems to have been the Tower of London, upon which was spent more than half of his office's total expenditure. A year after his initial appointment he was also placed in charge of St George's Chapel at Windsor which was '*en poynt du ruyne*'. He would have travelled continually, enduring the customary complaints of builders and the laziness or surliness of English workmen. He was once more at the heart of royal business.

Two or three events mark out his time as clerk. On 5 March 1390 a great storm destroyed many of the trees upon the royal estates, and there must have been further damage to buildings and outhouses; he would have been responsible for repairs, and for the sale of the fallen trees. A week after this tempest Chaucer was appointed to a commission to oversee the rebuilding of the walls and ditches beside the Thames, on what might be described as his home stretch between Woolwich and Greenwich.

In the summer of that year Chaucer also began work on building scaffolds and barriers for a great joust which at the king's command was to be held, at the beginning of October, in Smithfield to celebrate the newly established peace with France. It was a lavish affair preceded by the knights riding in procession, led 'by cheynes of gold' held by the ladies of the Garter whom Chaucer had celebrated in *The Legend of Good Women*. At a banquet to mark the close of the proceedings, the king, in full regalia, wore the crown. There were joustings and displays of horsemanship during the day, with public feastings in the evening. Chaucer's duties included the proper decoration of the scaffolds themselves, a decoration which may have included the emblem of the white hart which Richard II used for the first

Depiction of stonemasons

time during these proceedings. It was a piece of public theatre for which Chaucer was partly responsible.

A month before these events, however, he was involved in more ignominious affairs. While travelling between

Westminster and Eltham, with a large sum of money in his possession, he was robbed; the incident took place by the 'Fowl Oke' in the parish of Deptford. His horse and purse were taken, together with the sum of £20 6s 8d he was carrying for unspecified building works. He was fortunate to have escaped with his life, but his shock and anger were compounded by a further two robberies, in Westminster and at Hatcham in Surrey. They both took place on the same day, which suggests a well-arranged conspiracy to ambush Chaucer. He was known to carry large sums of money, to builders and to others, and it could not have been difficult to track his movements in Westminster and the adjacent countryside. He was then followed and robbed; ten pounds were taken from him at Westminster, and a little over nine pounds at Hatcham. This second bout of robberies was carried out by organised horse-thieves; that is perhaps why Chaucer escaped with his life.

A commission of enquiry was set up to investigate the affair, and eventually Chaucer was discharged of any responsibility for the money lost. One of the robbers, Richard Berelay, gave evidence against his companions on condition that the charges against him were dropped. But he had not reckoned on another device of the law. One of those whom he accused denied the charge and offered to defend himself by trial of battle. Berelay was duly defeated and, as a result, hanged. It is an example of those older forces at work within the practice of what is termed 'early modern law'. One of the others accused, Thomas Talbot alias 'Broad' or 'Brode', escaped the gallows on the grounds that he could read: he pleaded the privilege of a clerk, and was handed over as a 'convict clerk' to the archdeacon of York. It seems that another of those accused, William Huntingfield, also pleaded benefit of clergy (that he was literate) and was despatched to Marshalsea rather than the scaffold. Literacy was literally a saving grace. The convention emphasises the social significance of reading itself, in an era when Chaucer was turning from the oral delivery of the court to the relatively closed world of the book.

It is perhaps not coincidental that, less than a year after these robberies, Chaucer resigned his office as clerk. He may have expected an arduous appointment, but he could not have anticipated such a dangerous one. No doubt the continual pressure of business did play some part in his decision to resign; it must have seemed to him at the time that he had very little leisure left for his writing, especially in a period when he had embarked upon the long course of *The Canterbury Tales*.

It is sometimes surmised, however, that he was asked to resign due to some incapacity; there is some evidence to support this claim. An early audit of his office revealed that there had been an over-spending of some twenty pounds. His replacement, John Gedney, was a career civil servant who, on the evidence of the records, approached his duties with more fervour and energy than Chaucer himself.

Chaucer composed a short 'envoy' in this period which may bear some relation to his resignation:

> And but you list releve him of his peyne,
> Preyeth his beste frend of his noblesse
> That to som beter estat he may atteyne.

As a good and faithful servant of the crown, however, he was rewarded with a sinecure; in the same year he was given the post of sub-forester for the forest of North Petherton. It is perhaps hard to envisage the poet fulfilling the normal duties of a forester, but no such unlikely scenario needs to present itself. The rights to the land in question were then being debated in the courts and, since Chaucer knew both parties to the dispute, it is likely that he was engaged in the role of arbiter and negotiator during the proceedings. His skills in that area were sufficiently well known.

Yet he had now entered a period of semi-retirement after the busy activity of the previous two years. He had lost his large income as clerk of the king's works, and may have found it necessary to moderate his own expenditure. He still received the annuity of £10 first granted to him by John of Gaunt, and in the early months of 1392 he received a gift of £10 from the king '*pro regardo et bono servicio*'. Perhaps the royal household had heard of his straitened circumstances. Large debts owed to him by the exchequer, as a result of his work as clerk, were after some delay also repaid to him. Yet he was still obliged to borrow money on at least one occasion; in the summer of 1392 he borrowed 26s 8d for the period of one week. This puzzling short-term loan, by a professional money-lender named Henry Mawfield, cannot now be explained; but at least it confirms that Chaucer was not by any contemporaneous standard a wealthy man at this point in his life. In subsequent years he was also sued for small debts, but this is no real reflection upon his credit in any sense; he was merely part of the late medieval loan culture where such actions were commonplace.

He was in his late middle age and, unlike the more sprightly characters of *The Canterbury Tales*, beyond any prospect of love or marriage. In one of the short poems that Chaucer wrote in this period, 'Merciles Beaute', there is a wonderful evocation of his chastened but still ironic self:

> Love hath my name ystrike out of his sclat,
> And he is strike out of my bokes clene
> For evermo; ther is non other mene.
>> Sin I fro Love escaped am so fat,
>> I never thenk to ben in his prison lene;
>> Sin I am free, I counte him not a bene.

In the same period he addressed a verse letter to his friend and companion, the courtier Henry Scogan, in which he laments his situation at Greenwich by the mouth of the Thames:

> In th'ende of which strem I am dul as ded,
> Forgete in solytarie wildernesse . . .

There is an element of ritual complaint here, with its echo of Ovidian exile, but it is not hard to detect a current of true feeling running somewhere within it.

In the year of his retirement from the office of the king's works he occupied his unaccustomed leisure with the useful little treatise composed for the instruction and entertainment of his ten-year-old son Lewis. (See Chapter Seven.) It is entitled *A Treatise on the Astrolabe*, and has the merit of being the oldest surviving English handbook on the use of a scientific instrument – the astrolabe in question being an elaborately modelled sphere upon which the movements of the moon and planets can be traced. It was used for taking the altitude, or 'the heighte of any thing' as Chaucer puts it, and to solve certain practical problems concerned with astronomical observation. In *The Canterbury Tales*, for example, a poor Oxford scholar possesses 'His astrelabie, longynge for his art'.

At this late date it is not an easy book to read or

A philosopher teaching with the aid of an astrolabe

understand. Chaucer himself apologises in his prologue for 'curious endityng and hard sentence', yet clearly it was aimed at the comprehension of a ten-year-old medieval child. This in itself says much about the relative progress in human education.

Chaucer commences his work with a charming address. 'Lyte Lowys my sone, I apercyve wel by certeyne evydences thyn abilite to lerne sciences touching nombres and proporciouns; and as wel considre I thy besy praier in special to lerne the tretys of the Astrelabie.' The ensuing narrative has been described as the best example of medieval scientific prose in English, and certainly it bears witness to the fact that the poet was fully aware of all the developments in what he once called 'al this newe science that men lere'. He had a working knowledge of astrology as well as of astronomy, and the evidence of his allusions suggests that he was cognisant of modern medicine as well.

It has been suggested that in the year after his composition of *A Treatise on the Astrolabe* he wrote another treatise entitled *The Equatorie of the Planetis*, which is concerned with the geometrical calculation of the positions of the seven planets. This is of more uncertain provenance, however, and rests upon the notation of 'radix chaucer' beside the date of December 1392. It is also transcribed in a hand not unlike that of Chaucer himself, which adds more matter to the speculation. Whether composed by Chaucer or not, it is at least evidence of scientific writing in what might be called the 'circle' of the poet. Contemporaries such as Ralph Strode and John Gower were interested in the latest developments in astronomy or mathematics as a branch of general human education; they were not 'specialists' or 'professionals' in the sphere of knowledge, but part of an urban movement of learning. In that sense they were the precursors of the 'London humanists' of the late fifteenth century.

Yet his best remembered work was still to come. He had begun to compose the poems which make up *The Canterbury Tales* before he had taken up the post of clerk of the king's works, as we have seen, but in this period of half-retirement he had the leisure to contemplate his design. He was writing in Greenwich rather than in London, and as a result had formed a more general idea of any possible audience. There are also indications within the poem that its text was meant to be read and not heard. In 'The Second Nun's Prologue' he appeals to his putative reader:

> Yet preye I yow that reden that I write

and in 'The Miller's Prologue' he advises the same reader:

> And therfore, whoso list it nat yheere,
> Turne over the leef and chese another tale.

His muse is no longer one of performance and story-telling but of more measured effects and a more impersonal tone.

He may have worked upon more than one tale at a time. He left some unfinished, and revised others as he went along. Epilogues are cancelled, and prologues are rewritten. He took lines from one tale, and added them to another. He placed three or four tales within a coherent and dramatic arrangement, but left others stray and unattached. Certain

of the stories are appropriately matched with their speakers;
'The Canon's Yeoman's Tale' and 'The Pardoner's Tale',
for example, could only be narrated by those particular
individuals. But other tales bear no relation at all to their
ostensible source. 'The Nun's Priest's Tale' and 'The

Full page from *The Canterbury Tales*: 'The Pardoner's Tale'

Merchant's Tale' could have been narrated by any one of the pilgrims. There is internal evidence within 'The Shipman's Tale' that it was originally meant to be spoken by a woman. Other characters literally ride into the poem at a late stage, and are introduced casually within the narrative.

Some of the Canterbury pilgrims grew in stature and significance in the act of composition. Chaucer realised that he had created a wonderfully emblematic character in 'The Wife of Bath's Prologue', so he increased her role within the larger poem; he added new lines about her at a later date, and introduced references to her in 'The Clerk's Tale' and 'The Merchant's Tale' as a way of affirming her identity. It is not unusual for a writer to realise the force of a character after it has been created, and to treat that character as a phenomenon in the world. Hence in one verse epistle he advises a friend:

> The Wyf of Bathe I pray yow that ye rede
> Of this matere that we have on honde.

The Canterbury Tales is so inclusive a poem that fictional characters become real and real people become fictional. The Host, Herry Bailey, was a contemporary Southwark landlord well known to Londoners; the Cook is more than likely based upon Roger of Ware, otherwise known as 'Hogge of Ware', a famous cook of the period. And there is a punning reference in the 'General Prologue' to a sergeant-at-law:

> Therto he koude endite and make a thyng,
> Ther koude no wight pynche at his writyng.

Here 'pynche' seems to allude to Thomas Pynchbeck, a sergeant-at-law with whom Chaucer had less than friendly relations. Chaucer seems deliberately to efface or to ignore the boundaries between life and art. The poem is inconsistent and inconclusive precisely because it represents the condition of life itself.

That is why Chaucer himself enters the poem in a direct way. This was not a new device; both Langland and Gower make use of autobiographical references. But no poet before Chaucer created as substantial, or as dramatic, a persona. He becomes one of the pilgrims. The Man of Law, in the course of the journey to Canterbury, has cause to mention Chaucer's poetry:

> I kan right now no thrifty tale seyn
> That Chaucer, thogh he kan but lewedly
> On metres and on rymyng craftily,
> Hath seyd hem in swich Englissh as he kan . . .

The poet himself is addressed by Herry Bailey in less than flattering terms:

> Thou lookest as thou woldest fynde an hare,
> For evere upon the ground I se thee stare.

Chaucer presents himself as portly, distracted and a little obtuse. It is his usual technique, one meant to disarm criticism and to inspire comedy. His own contributions to *The Canterbury Tales*, however, are somewhat puzzling. The first, 'Sir Thopas', is a parody of minor English romances. The second, 'The Tale of Melibee', is a lengthy prose translation of a French allegory on the theme of patience or 'mesure'; it may even have been completed, for other purposes, at an earlier date. By placing himself within the narrative, however, Chaucer renders the poem more 'real' and more credible.

Yet reality changes. However tempting it may be to claim *The Canterbury Tales* as a work of naturalism, a piece of native realism consonant with the infancy of the language (as fresh as Chaucer's favourite flower, the daisy), it must be resisted. The poem takes its place among the other artefacts of the period, and can only properly be understood in relation to them. Thus the art of the Ricardian court, for example, conveys a new interest in crowded scenes and realistic detail; late fourteenth-century tapestries are more concerned with continuous narrative as well as free-standing and naturalistic figures; the manuscript illuminations of the period display a new emphasis upon delicately rendered natural scenery and realistic architectural backgrounds; painting and sculpture are concerned with individual expression and more finely rendered attempts at facial modelling. There was also a more general concern with the vivid depiction of emotion, particularly of pathos and grief. In the altar panels of the period, such as those preserved in Norwich Cathedral, the elaborate patterning of the surface does not preclude the inventive use of facial expression or particular detail. None of these developments needs to have affected *The Canterbury Tales* in a direct fashion, but they suggest that the poem is part of a family of contemporaneous concerns.

There is also the matter of form. In recent years the peculiar fragmentary quality of the narrative, as well as its sudden juxtapositions of meaning, have been explained as examples of the Gothic mode. The use of an open-ended and continuous narrative, recounting the stages in a progress or on a journey, is an essential element in Gothic narrative whether sculpted out of stone or words; the combination or translation of secular and spiritual material, often accomplished by an exaggerated mixture of styles, is another manifestation of the Gothic sensibility. It is exemplified by Chaucer's mingling of bawdy fabliaux and religious allegories. A less theoretical model can also be adduced here. Some of the most influential works of the period were conceived as framed collections of stories – Ovid's *Metamorphoses* and Boccaccio's *Decameron* are examples ancient and modern. In Chaucer's lifetime there was also a fashion for collections of material in one volume, which acted as a kind of family album; sermons and tales and jokes and moral exempla were placed side by side within the leaves of one manuscript to be perused and read at leisure. *The Canterbury Tales* can be seen as an aspect of that tradition.

But nothing can prepare the reader for the sheer force and variety of Chaucer's poem. It opens with a celebration of the coming of the spring, which invokes the sacred and secular elements of that season; it is an opposition and a contrast which will be repeated throughout the long journey of the pilgrims towards Canterbury. The 'General Prologue' itself may not have been written by Chaucer at the beginning of the enterprise, but it is the best possible introduction to the poet's methods. It begins in a familiar and recognisable place:

In Southwerk at the Tabard as I lay

but opens out into a general view of late medieval society. Chaucer introduces himself – or his narrator – while at the same time outlining the circumstances of the poem. Some pilgrims have gathered at Southwark and, in order to pass the time on their way to Canterbury, agree to narrate various stories; the one judged to be the best story-teller, the purveyor of 'best sentence and moost solaas', will be given a meal at the expense of the rest.

The idea of a pilgrimage as narrative device seems to be original to Chaucer. It is in fact a wonderful invention, for which he must have seen the possibilities at once. It affords a frame for many distinct characters and tales, but it also provides a spiritual context of unequalled authority; life itself was often seen as a pilgrimage, as it is eloquently revealed in 'The Knight's Tale':

> This world nys but a thurghfare ful of wo
> And we been pilgrymes, passynge to and fro.

So the journey to Canterbury, the 'hooly blisful martir for to seke', can be used to sublimate or at least excuse the most unholy material. If Chaucer ever looked up from his books into the world, there were examples very close to home: Greenwich itself was on the route of the Canterbury pilgrims, as has been observed, and he would have encountered groups of them at all times of the day.

The 'General Prologue' introduces a variety of pilgrims, including Chaucer and the Host of the gathering, who are really to be numbered according to the diversity of their professions and social status. The description of the salacious Wife of Bath precedes that of the holy Parson, that of the Shipman comes before the Doctor of Physick. In medieval fashion they are at once highly individualised and typically representative. That is why the poem itself has been seen both as a drama of various characters and as a refined form of 'estates satire' in which characters speak according to their 'degree' or role in life. As Thomas Speght, one of Chaucer's first editors and biographers, put it, the tales exemplify 'the state of the Church, the Court and the Country, with such arte and cunning, that although none could deny himself to be touched, yet none durst complaine that he was wronged'. This suggests too much prior construction on Chaucer's part, and of course disregards many of his specifically urban preoccupations, but it touches upon an important truth. Chaucer is as concerned with the type as with the person; he creates figures whose fidelity to the truths of observed experience is matched by an awareness of their general place in the scheme of things. The Monk is 'ful fat and in good poynt' but he also represents the cupidity and corruption of the Church. The Wife of Bath is a formidable matron, but she is also 'larger than life' in the sense that she represents the corruption of womankind after the negligence of Eve. This correspondence does not apply to all of the pilgrims – it is hard to see what the Shipman and the Reeve represent in general terms – but there is throughout the poem an implied debate between formal or typical roles and real conduct. The poem is conceived as a set of dramatic debates and interventions, but it also takes as its larger theme the nature of a threatened and disrupted social order. Although Chaucer himself rarely alludes to the state of the world around him, it could be adduced from *The Canterbury Tales* that he was living in a most confused and disordered society. The papacy was in disarray, the relations between Church and State continually questioned, the governance of the country perilously poised between the king and recalcitrant nobles. Historians often point to the Hundred Years' War and the Peasants' Revolt as the evidence for malaise and disruption. We may also find it in the revelations of the Friar and the Pardoner, the Wife of Bath and the Summoner.

The first of the sequence, 'The Knight's Tale', was in fact written before Chaucer ever contemplated *The Canterbury Tales* and was placed within the frame as a story almost perfect of its kind and eminently well suited to the 'verray,

'Here begynneth the knightes tale', woodcut illustrating a book by William Caxton, *c.*1434

parfit gentil knyght' described in the 'General Prologue'. It is a retelling of a chivalric romance set in the landscape of that classical and almost mythic past which 'olde stories' inhabit, and is concerned with the woeful adventures of Palamon and Arcite for the hand of Emelye. The traditional mixture of arms and love is here modified by Chaucer's reading of Boethius, so that the larger theme becomes one of fate and human destiny. Yet even here Chaucer's scepticism inevitably plays a part; the tale itself has been interpreted both as a relatively straightforward celebration of valour and chivalry, befitting the social and moral status of the Knight, and as a satire on the sanguinary and mercenary truth of knighthood in the late middle ages. It is a tribute, at least, to the essential ambiguity of Chaucer's somewhat detached tone.

That detachment is nowhere more obvious than in his decision to follow this tale of high romance with an obscene farce. 'The Miller's Tale' is connected with 'The Knight's Tale' by a prologue in which Chaucer displays his skills as a writer of comic dialogue, the Miller declares:

'For I wol speke or elles go my wey.'
Oure Hoost answerde, 'Tel on, a devel wey!
Thou art a fool; thy wit is overcome.'
'Now herkneth,' quod the Millere, 'alle and some!'

The Miller 'for dronken was al pale' but, more importantly, he 'is a cherl'. His story is narrated in the terms of a cherl; it is composed in the same decasyllabic couplets as those of 'The Knight's Tale' but its vocabulary and cadence are quite differently conceived. It is a 'low' story of illicit sex replete with intimate matters:

> Derk was the nyght as pich, or as the cole,
> And at the wyndow out she putte hir hole.

It represents the broad sexual humour which the English have always enjoyed, but in this instance the salacious farce is part of a story which parodies the formulae of the mystery plays; it is in effect a comic rendition of Noah's Flood. There is perhaps no better example of the way in which buffoonery and obscenity can coexist with sacred subjects. There is another comic point here, since 'The Miller's Tale' effectively satirises the courtly love of 'The Knight's Tale'; Chaucer is setting up an ironical dialogue within his own poem.

'The Miller's Tale' is in turn parodied by 'The Reeve's Tale'. This succeeding story recounts the cuckolding of a miller not unlike the one on Chaucer's pilgrimage, and also places the sexual adventures in a much more crude and mechanical setting. It is a fine example of the fabliau, a form derived from the French but deepened by Chaucer's concern for characterisation and by his unequalled gifts of mimicry; in the poem he adopts a Northern accent for two young scholars who were born

> Fer in the north; I kan nat telle where.

It is plain enough that the poet introduced the characters precisely in order to imitate or indeed create a northern dialect:

> Oure manciple, I hope he wil be deed,
> Swa werkes ay the wanges in his heed.

The last line can be translated, roughly, thus: 'So ache the teeth in his head'. It suggests Chaucer's continual search for novelty and freshness of expression, and his constant inventiveness in pursuit of diverse speech. His 'ear' was as good and as alert as ever.

'The Reeve's Tale' is in a sense completed by 'The Cook's Tale', a short and rather inglorious tale of an apprentice who 'dwelled in oure citee'. Like a character out of Hogarth, but already an urban type by the fourteenth century, the 'prentys' wastes his master's time in game and riot until he is discharged; he then consorts with thieves:

> And hadde a wyf that heeld for contenance
> A shoppe, and swyved for hir sustenance.

His wife, in other words, was a prostitute. The tale ends there; it is apparently incomplete but in fact it may represent a subtle gradation of love's joys from the chivalric courtliness of the Knight to the low pleasures of the urban poor. These poems were indeed written in sequence, and it is possible to see Chaucer changing his language subtly from one to the other so that he can present a panoply of stylistic effects. It is both an experiment, and an innovation, in English letters.

'The Man of Law's Tale', which in most editions of the poem follows the 'love sequence', is composed in the more formal and elaborate 'rime royal' stanza; it is a Christian romance based upon the piety and patience of Constance who follows 'The wyl of Crist' through the most extreme misfortunes. Chaucer is in one sense limning a portrait of late medieval piety, which in large part extolled the virtues of female suffering and female martyrdom. The great religious writers of Chaucer's own period, Julian of Norwich and Margery Kempe, were female; the strain of affective female piety is particularly strong in fourteenth-century devotional texts. The image of Constance is the image of the age.

She is, however, well matched by the Wife of Bath who in most collections now follows. Her prologue is one of the most famous passages in all English literature where, in a language borrowed from scholastics and wise clerks, she justifies her belief that:

> Experience, though noon auctoritee
> Were in this world, is right ynogh for me
> To speke of wo that is in mariage.

Chaucer also uses much of the anti-feminist literature of the period but, by placing it in the Wife's capacious mouth, he lends it a new and ironical lease of life. He is a great magpie of other men's words, but has learned the trick of dramatising them through the medium of a vivid persona. Many scholars have concerned themselves with the sources and origins of this prologue and tale – from St Paul to the *Roman de la rose* – but the great attribute of Chaucer's language is its freshness.

'The Wife of Bath's Tale' is followed by a pair of connected and contrasting stories, narrated in turn by the Friar and the Summoner. 'The Summoner's Tale' is in fact interrupted in dramatic fashion:

'Nay, ther thou lixt, thou Somonour!' quod the Frere.
'Pees,' quod oure Hoost, 'for Cristes mooder deere!'

Part of the apparent realism of Chaucer's method lies in his willingness to subvert narrative conventions in this manner; it is part of the novelty of his enterprise. A summoner was one who called guilty or suspected parties to the local ecclesiastical court; it was a generally hated profession, since those who espoused it were known for their mendacity and corruption. Friars in turn were popularly regarded as greedy and sexually voracious. In pitting them against each other, then, Chaucer is making a more general statement about the worldliness and frailty of the Church. This does not make him a Wycliffite or proto-Protestant, as some commentators have suggested, but, more importantly, a contemporary ironist and satirist.

The two stories which follow have been designated by scholars as 'Fragment IV' or 'Group E' as a way of bringing order to Chaucer's apparent disorderliness. 'The Clerk's Tale' is a story of wifely patience and fidelity in the face of her husband's brutal testing of her obedience; it will not appeal to modern taste, perhaps, but Chaucer seems preoccupied with the sorrows of the female. It is related to what can only be called his benignity, as summarised by the proverb he uses more than once. 'Pitee', he writes, 'renneth soone in gentil herte.' 'The Merchant's Tale' offers another perspective on the matter, with the story of a young wife trapped in a repugnant marriage with an elderly knight. After they have been to bed for the first time:

> The slakke skyn aboute his nekke shaketh
> Whil that he sang, so chaunteth he and craketh.

It is not a pretty picture. The wife has her revenge, however, in the most bawdy and explicit manner. Chaucer feels obliged to apologise for his obscenity – 'I kan nat glose, I am a rude man' – but of course he revels in it. It is in any case an important part of the medieval imagination. In a similar context the romance of 'The Squire's Tale' is contrasted with the supernaturalism of 'The Franklin's Tale'; they are a reflection of the medieval taste for the marvellous in all of its guises.

It would be otiose to describe in detail each of the tales, but there are specific points of interest. One of the tales delivered by Chaucer himself, in his guise as narrator, is the first literary parody in the English language; 'Chaucers Tale of Thopas' is a pastiche of early English romances which were composed in what are known as 'tail-rhyme' stanzas. Chaucer perfectly catches the elliptical and formulaic gabble of these old stories:

> Yborn he was in fer contree,
> In Flaundres, al biyonde the see,
> At Poperyng, in the place.
> His fader was a man ful free,
> And lord he was of that contree,
> As it was Goddes grace.

It has been said that you can only parody successfully writing which you love or admire and, on that basis, it is not difficult to see why he chose this particular form for his attention.

These romances, collected in endless manuscript versions, would have been the staple of Chaucer's early reading; they would certainly have provided an introduction to native English poetry, and in his parodic return to these beginnings there is an implied reflection on the measure of his own poetic achievement in that language. That is nowhere better expressed than in 'The Nun's Priest's Tale', a beast fable taken from French sources but handled with such diversity and humour that it becomes a model of well-constructed artifice. The story of Chauntecleer and Pertelote is delivered in a mock-heroic style which is perfectly balanced between bathos and the sublime; farce and learning, confusion and fluency, are mingled together in one of Chaucer's most accomplished stories.

The Canterbury Tales ends with a short prose treatise, 'The Parson's Tale', which is in essence a disquisition on the nature and effect of penitence. It is concluded with a retraction by Chaucer himself of 'my translacions and enditynges of worldly vanitees' including *Troilus and Criseyde* and even 'the tales of Caunterbury, thilke that sownen into synne'. It has been hard for some critics to interpret this. If *The Canterbury Tales* were solely a work of literary art, in the modern sense, then the treatise and the retraction appear to be redundant. But that is merely a contemporary preoccupation. There was really no such thing as 'literature' but, rather, various models of the world and mirrors of human conduct. In that context 'The Parson's Tale' is perhaps the inevitable conclusion of a poem which has emphasised the frailty of humankind. It is in fact a translation, from two Latin originals that have been stitched together, which in turn suggests that we cannot see

The Canterbury Tales as a work of personal or private expression. The 'retraction' of his works was a familiar and pious convention, for example, which would guarantee the seriousness of his intent; it is no more an expression of his private wishes than the narrator of the poem is an accurate representation of the poet himself. That is why *The Canterbury Tales* is in many respects almost an impersonal work. Despite its irony and its frequent obscenity, its moments of low drama and its passages of spirited comedy, it has the distance and the detachment of great art. William Blake understood this quality very well when he wrote, in a descriptive catalogue, that

> the characters of Chaucer's Pilgrims are the characters which compose all ages and nations: as one age falls, another rises, different to mortal sight, but to immortals only the same; for we see the same characters repeated again and again, in animals, vegetables, minerals, and in men; nothing new occurs in identical existence; Accident ever varies, Substance can never suffer change nor decay.

Chaucer himself is 'the great poetical observer of men, who in every age is born to record and eternize its acts'.

'Accident', however, lies in the world of time through which humankind passes in its pilgrimage. That is why on one level *The Canterbury Tales* is an experiment in diversity, a poem devoted to the celebration of variety and change. In a world which is mutable and flawed the most important characteristics are likely to be those of variation and surprise. From various tales comes the experience of heterogeneity.

As Chaucer puts it on a number of occasions, 'Diverse folk diversely they said', 'Diverse men diverse thynges seyden' and 'Al be it told somtyme in sondry wyse / Of sondry folk'. It is the philosophical principle within the poem, if the anachronism can be permitted, given expression in many different ways. He created diversity, too, from the mixing of French or Latin loan-words with Anglo-Saxon diction. It has already been noticed how he contrasts saint's tale with indecent fabliau, just as on the pilgrimage itself he brings together prioress and cook, 'churls' and 'gentils'. Some tales also include apparently incompatible elements within one narrative. Chaucer also created a format in which the old tales – the legends and the myths and the stories – could be given a fresh access of life by being narrated in novel circumstances and by a multitude of different people. The apparent 'realism' of the narrative, celebrated by writers and critics, is generated by this diversity; by creating a number of lives and of stories it mimics the relative variety of life itself. That is its charm, and its achievement.

Chapter Twelve
Last Years

There are more than eighty extant manuscripts of *The Canterbury Tales*, all of them compiled after Chaucer's death, which testify to the immediate popularity of the long poem. In the last years of his life he may have circulated individual tales, or bundles of tales, to his friends and contemporaries; one or two may have found their way to the court. He had not lost all contact with that world. The evidence of his various appearances as a 'witness' indicates his residence in Kent; he was present both at Woolwich and at Combe, no doubt for a fee, to witness charters of release and transfers of property. He was also appointed by a local landowner, Gregory Ballard, to act as his attorney. But the royal associations were kept in place. At the beginning of 1392 Richard II awarded him ten pounds for good service; this suggests, although it does not prove, that Chaucer was still engaged in some form of royal employment. No evidence of this has ever come to light, but it might be related to some duties in Kent itself.

On 28 February 1394 Richard II bestowed upon Chaucer an annual grant of twenty pounds '*pro bono servicio*'; this was in effect a pension, renewing that which Chaucer had sold to John Scalby six years before. There are several records of Chaucer asking for a 'prest' or advance upon the annuity, however, which suggests that he was not necessarily

living in affluence; in the same period, too, he was sued for
the recovery of a debt of some fourteen pounds. In 1397 the
king also granted Chaucer, as a good and faithful public
servant, a tun or large cask of wine each year; in the manner
of all bureaucracies the gift was not presented on time, and
in the following year Chaucer petitioned the exchequer on
his own behalf for delivery of the wine.

The award of the exchequer annuity, however, was not
necessarily an indication of complete retirement; the terms
of the grant itself suggested further public service '*in
futurum*'. That was not necessarily an idle or conventional
formula. In 1398 Chaucer was given a 'safe conduct' for the
pursuit of the king's 'arduous and urgent business' over a
period of two years; the nature of his mission is unknown,
but it does not seem to have involved any journey overseas.
It may have been a procedure, however, to protect Chaucer
from any legal action concerning his debts. It is at least an
indication that the poet was still noticed by the authorities,
as a man either to be defended or to be summoned on the
king's behalf. As visible proof of his merit Chaucer was also
rewarded by Henry Bolingbroke with a scarlet gown lined
with fur, before his benefactor came to the throne as Henry
IV. Chaucer was still a 'high person'.

He was, in any case, about to leave Kent and to return to
London. He may have grown tired of the relative quiet of
the country and longed once more for the noise and bustle
of the city. He was coming to the end of his life, and wished
to return to his origin. He may simply have grown restless.
It has often been said by poets and artists that a change of
scene materially helps the process of composition. He
returned to the city in 1398, two years before his death, and

in the following year took out a fifty-three-year lease upon a 'tenement' in the garden of the Lady Chapel of the abbey in the adjacent city of Westminster. He was in possession of a small but comfortable house, with garden, in the precincts of a great and ancient church; it may have seemed to him a place conducive to the further writing of *The Canterbury Tales*. The length of the lease is perhaps odd in a man of advancing years, but it may have been a legal fiction. It was the equivalent of 'grace and favour' accommodation, since the same house had in the past been leased to retired royal servants. It was part of the area of the abbey's sanctuary, but that does not necessarily mean that it was a sheltered or secluded spot. The poet would have seen from his window the south transept of the abbey, but he was in the immediate vicinity of the White Rose tavern which was also in sanctuary grounds.

In the autumn of 1399 Richard II was forced to abdicate by the superior forces of Henry Bolingbroke, who had returned from exile in France with the express purpose of over-throwing the king of England. When he ascended to the throne as Henry IV, however, the new king renewed Chaucer's annuity and confirmed the earlier grant of a cask of wine; Chaucer also received an additional payment of forty marks (approximately twenty-seven pounds) as a sign of royal favour. It may be an indication of the poet's relative lack of sigificance. It suggests the impersonality of the bureaucracy around kings, when a major shift of loyalty can be regarded simply as a change of employer. But it also suggests Chaucer's modest or noncommittal deportment in the affairs of state, that he could be regarded as '*dilectus armiger noster*' by both sovereigns: his long-time benefactor Richard II, and also the man who overthrew Richard in order to make himself Henry IV.

There was in fact a delay in the payments, and the sudden lack of funds prompted Chaucer to address a begging poem to the new king entitled 'The Complaint of Chaucer to his Purse':

> To yow, my purse, and to noon other wight
> Complayne I, for ye be my lady dere.
> I am so sory, now that ye been lyght . . .
> For I am shave as nye as any frere.

So Chaucer had returned to the city of his birth or, more precisely, to the city of Westminster further along the Thames. He was, in theory, sufficiently well rewarded for his years of service. The last two payments of his annuity were not made to him in person, however, which may suggest that he was already in ill-health. One account by the sixteenth-century antiquarian, Leland, suggests that the poet 'grew old and white-haired'; he was now approaching sixty, not an advanced age but in a period of chronic illness and sudden death a respectable one. Leland also relates how Chaucer believed 'old age itself to be a sickness', but that may simply be a chronicler's commonplace.

There are apocryphal references to Chaucer's last years in an account which suggests that, before his death, Chaucer cried out 'Woe is me! Woe is me!' in regret for the bawdy poems that he had written. Since he had already composed a public retraction, such private grief seems unlikely. It has in fact been suggested that the last work he ever completed on *The Canterbury Tales* concerned the obscene tales of 'Group A', from the Miller, the Reeve and the Cook. It would be a fitting end to the career of a quintessentially urban writer.

The cause and manner of his death are not known; he expired, however, in a year of plague. The generally accepted date, 25 October 1400, was taken from the inscription upon a tombstone erected some 150 years later. That tomb rests in the south transept of Westminster Abbey, now known as 'Poets' Corner'. Originally Geoffrey Chaucer was buried in an obscure site, generally left for monastic officials, by the entrance to St Benedict's Chapel; he seems to have been granted no elaborate service or ceremonial, but to have been buried as the role and rank of a minor court servant deserved. He remained circumspect, and reticent, until the end.

Chaucer's tomb, in Poets' Corner, Westminster Abbey

Selected Reading

Primary Sources
The Riverside Chaucer, new edn. Edited by Larry D. Benson (Boston, 1987).

Chaucer Life-Records. Edited by Martin M. Crow and Clair C. Olson (Oxford, 1966).

Secondary Sources
The Cambridge Chaucer Companion. Edited by Piero Boitani and Jill Mann (Cambridge, 1986).

A Guide to Chaucer's Language. Written by David Burnley (London, 1983).

Chaucer: His Life, His Works, His World. Written by Donald R. Howard (New York, 1987).

Who Murdered Chaucer? A Medieval Mystery. Written by Terry Jones and others (London, 2003).

The Life of Geoffrey Chaucer. Written by Derek Pearsall (Oxford, 1992).

Companion to Chaucer Studies. Edited by Beryl Rowland (Oxford, 1979).

The Personality of Chaucer. Written by Edward Wagenknecht (Oklahoma, 1968).

Translations of the Quoted Material

13   There came a stealthy thief named Death, that in this country all the people slayeth.

17   He was singing or fluting all the day, he could write the words and music of songs.

19   . . . the roaring of the stone, when it is propelled from the device.

20   Of them that make the martial sound of trumpet, horn and bugle; for in fighting and bloodshed the clarion call is employed with delight.

23   Of masters he had more than thrice ten that were expert and knowledgeable in law.

24   'Ha! ha!' he cried, 'For the passion of Christ this miller received a sharp reply to the question of lodgings!'

32   O true light of eyes that are blind, o true object of desire for those who labour or who are in distress . . .

34   It is the Romance of the Rose, in which I include all the arts of love.

Though we call them mermaids in English, as is our custom, in France they are called sirens.

Generosity was always in her mind so that she was both honourable and liberal in her conduct. She was another Alexander, she derived most pleasure, in fact, when she gave a present and said 'Take this'.

36   For the love of God don't believe that I say anything from any evil intent. But I must repeat all of their tales, whether better or worse . . . Do not blame me if you make the wrong choice.

38 She was so gracious that she was the most constant, and had the most gentle and moderate disposition, that I have ever encountered – so entirely patient was her mind.

51 For when your work is done, and you have finished all your sums, instead of getting rest and entertainment you go back home straight away and there, dumb as any stone, you sit down to another book until you are quite out of it.

55 'In the suburbs of a town,' he said, 'lurking in bye-ways and blind alleys, where thieves and robbers instinctively live secretly and in fear.'

56 The keeper of the gates began to call out to the people who were outside the gates, and instructed them to drive in their animals or else spend the night out there.

59 Yes, God knows, you yourself have sixty books both old and new – all of them filled with excellent stories.

60 And if old books did not exist, then the key to memory itself would be lost.
For out of old fields, as men say, comes all the new corn from year to year.
All his books, great and small, including a treatise on astronomy, were kept on shelves at the head of his bed.

69 Great Barnabo Visconti from Milan, the god of pleasure and the scourge of Lombardy.
And be not like the tyrants of Lombardy.

72 'But he seemed to be a man of great authority . . .'

73 Of trust, of fear, of jealousy, of judgement, of success, and of folly.

74 It was of gold and shone so brightly that men had never seen such a sight – it was as if the sky had won another golden sun, so shone the bright feathers of the eagle, and now it began gently to descend.
Now listen everyone that can understand English.

75 You go to great trouble to praise his skill, although you play no part in it.

76 I saw him put a windmill under a walnut shell.

77 I have no such intention, I promise you! I am quite content that no man has possession of my name. I know best how I stand.

78 The art of poetry would be displayed here, if the verse were not so facile and uncouth . . .

87 For you have lost the taste of love, I suppose, as a sick man can no longer distinguish between the sweet and the bitter. But nevertheless although you are out of action, you can say even if you cannot do. Many men like to watch the wrestling even if they could not take part in the contest.

88 The life is short, and the art so hard to learn, the attempt is so hard, the victory so difficult.

89 The goose, the cuckoo and the duck all cried out, 'Kek kek!', 'Cuckoo!' and 'Quack! Quack!' . . .
Now welcome summer with your soft sun that has overcome the winter storms, and driven away the long dark nights!

95 Reserved their shrillest cries when they were killing the Flemings.

96 O stormy people! unstable and always untrue! as injudicious and as changing as a weather-vane! delighting in any new sensation. Like the moon you wax and wane!

102 You stand very high in her judgement, in a place worthy of your virtue . . .

104 Men say – I do not – that she gave him her heart.

107 You know the concealed qualities of things, about which people often wonder.
The nearer the fire the hotter it becomes – I believe everyone in this company knows this.
In truth I have never heard it mentioned in a story before – and no-one here has, I bet.

109 You, reader, you can well understand how my abilities cannot describe such misery . . .
Adam the scribe, if ever it so happens that you are asked to write out a new copy of Troilus or Boethius, you must transcribe more correctly my words – or else I wish you to get the scab under your long hair.

110 Go little book, go my little tragedy, and I hope that God sends your maker the strength to write a comedy before he dies. Little book do not contend with any others but be a willing subject of poetry itself. Kiss the steps where you see walk Virgil, Ovid, Homer, Lucan and Statius.

112 And when this book is completed present it on my behalf to the queen, either at the palaces of Eltham or of Sheen.

118 Here's Deptford, and it's already seven thirty in the morning! And here's Greenwich, where live many a shrew. It is high time you began your tale.

120 O prince, desire to be honourable. Cherish your people and hate extortion.

Here is no home, here is nothing but a wilderness: Go forth, pilgrim! Go forth, beast, out of your stall!

122 And greet Chaucer warmly when you meet him. He is my disciple and my poet.

123 And so you may see an example; trust no one in love – no one, that is, but me.

And if there is a false lover in this house – well, he behaved in the same way.

124 'Get lost, Jason! Now your horn is blown!'

125 And if you want to know who has travelled with him, go and read the Argonauticon – you will find a long enough story there.

126 But he is used to writing books and does not really care what subject matter he uses. That is the way he wrote the Romance of the Rose as well as Troilus and Cressida – he was an innocent, and didn't know what he was saying. In any case someone asked him to compose those two books, and he dared not refuse.

131 And so we agreed to get up early, to make our way there as I will now explain to you.

136 And if you wish to relieve him of his burden, pray his best friend from his nobility of character that he may attain to some better estate.

138 Love has struck my name from his slate, and in turn he has been taken off my books for good; there is no other way. And since from love I am escaped so plump, I have no thought of being incarcerated in his narrow prison; since I am free I don't think he's worth bothering with.

At the end of which stream I am as good as dead, forgotten in this lonely wilderness.

141   Yet I appeal to you who read what I write.
      And so whoever does not want to hear it, just turn the page and
      choose another tale.

143   I pray you, read the Wife of Bath on the subject we are now
      discussing.
      So he could draw up and write out a document, and there was
      no one who could find fault with what he had done.

144   I cannot tell you any profitable story that Chaucer, albeit he can
      only handle metre and rhyme in a slovenly way, has not already
      narrated in the best English he can muster.
      You look as if you are searching for a hare, for I always see you
      staring upon the ground.

146   In Southwark at the Tabard Inn as I lay.

147   This world is but a thoroughfare of woe, and we are all pilgrims
      passing to and fro.

150   'For I will speak or else go my own way.' And our host answered,
      'Go on, and the devil take you! You are a fool, and your wit is
      soaked in drink.' 'Now listen,' said the Miller, 'all of you!'

151   The night was as black as pitch or as a piece of coal. And out of
      the window she put her hole.
      Far in the north – I can't tell where.
      I expect our Manciple will be dead, so ache the teeth in his head.

152   He had a wife who for appearance sake kept a shop, but she had
      sex to make her money.

153   Experience, although it is not considered to be an authority in
      this world, is good enough for me to speak of all the trouble
      that comes with marriage.

154   'No. That is where you are lying, Summoner!' said the Friar.
      'Peace,' exclaimed our host, 'for Mary's sake!'

155   The slack skin about his neck shook when he sang, so did he
      chant and croak.
      He was born in a far country, in Flanders, way beyond the sea,
      in a place called Poperyng. His father was a great man, and was
      the lord of that country according to God's grace.

162   I will complain to you, my purse, and to no one else, for you
      are my dear lady. I am so sorry to see you in such a light
      condition . . . I am shaved as close as any friar.

Index

www.randomhouse.co.uk/vintage